Passions and Politics

Passions and Politics

Paul Ginsborg
Sergio Labate

Translated by David Broder

polity

First published in Italian as *Passioni e politica* © Giulio Einaudi editore s.p.a., Turin, 2016

This English edition copyright © Paul Ginsborg and Sergio Labate, 2019

The authors gratefully acknowledge the contribution of the University of Macerata to the translation costs of this work.

Polity Press
65 Bridge Street
Cambridge CB2 1UR, UK

Polity Press
101 Station Landing
Suite 300
Medford, MA 02155, USA

ISBN-13: 978-1-5095-3273-5
ISBN-13: 978-1-5095-3274-2 (pb)

A catalogue record for this book is available from the British Library.

Typeset in 11 on 14 pt Sabon by Servis Filmsetting Ltd, Stockport, Cheshire
Printed and bound in the United Kingdom by Clays Ltd, Elcograf S.p.A.

The publisher has used its best endeavours to ensure that the URLs for external websites referred to in this book are correct and active at the time of going to press. However, the publisher has no responsibility for the websites and can make no guarantee that a site will remain live or that the content is or will remain appropriate.

Every effort has been made to trace all copyright holders, but if any have been overlooked the publisher will be pleased to include any necessary credits in any subsequent reprint or edition.

For further information on Polity, visit our website: politybooks.com

To Daniele, who comes from Vinca

Contents

Acknowledgements

This short book is the fruit of dialogue and collaboration between a historian and a philosopher (both of whom seem to have emerged miraculously unscathed from the experience). They assume a shared responsibility for the whole text. It being the convention to attribute particular parts of the book to individual authors, pp. 1–14, 31–51, 95–120 can be attributed to Paul Ginsborg and pp. 15–30, 52–94, 121–6 to Sergio Labate.

Lastly, we would like to thank Chiara Stefani for her valuable help in preparing this text.

Paul Ginsborg and Sergio Labate
28 February 2016

Introduction

Boys, girls and a dog in front of Vinca Cemetery

August bank holiday 2015, in a village in the Apuan Alps. In the summer of 1944 Vinca was one of the small Tuscan settlements to be most tragically hit by the SS death squads, actively supported by the local Fascist *milizia* from Carrara. They shot around 170 people, most of them women and children, over the three days between 24 and 26 August. The Nazi-fascists packed twenty-nine women and their children into a little sheep pen called Il Mandrione. Insensitive to the cries, the begging and the tears of their victims, they gunned down every one of them.

Seventy-one years later, the village was full of people. This was quite a rare occurrence, given that small settlements like Vinca have suffered a second, demographic death – obviously a less terrible death than that inflicted by the SS, but a no less lethal one.[1] Visitors of Vinchese extraction come back to spend the weekend in houses that are left abandoned from one August to the next, former homes of the families who left the village in the years following the massacre. They come in their cars, many of them black and shiny vehicles with chrome wheelrims, rather too big for the size of the village itself. An occasional flash of wealth, if a modest one. There's quite a hubbub; on the church square people are playing tombola and a group of drunken male youth tell anyone within earshot that they need to 'have a piss'. All this seems quite normal; or is it?

Heading away from the medieval centre of the village, we come across a quite different scene. Five or six youngsters of both sexes are sitting in the lane in front of the cemetery. They are very young, perhaps sixteen or seventeen years old, and probably still in school. There is a big dog with them, tame and affectionate, with its paw in one of the girls' hands. This is a relaxed, tranquil group, *set apart*. We say hello and say how much we like the dog, which they are rather pleased about; but we don't stop to chat. Only later do we wish that we had done so. It would have been nice to ask them what they were doing, whether they had perhaps a grandmother or great-grandmother killed in the massacre, whether they thought that the passions that led to that act of unspeakable cruelty – first and foremost, the hatred and disdain for human life – could reappear, as history suggests. Who knows whether the kids in front of the gates of Vinca Cemetery, and all those like them, are aware of the great threats that loom over us like black clouds, the first signs of a storm ready to wipe out our civic coexistence and our democracy. Thinking back to that group, tender and reflective to all appearances, there comes to mind another group – the Turin youth who were to join the anti-fascist Resistance of

the Second World War. Natalia Ginzburg recalled how
at a certain point her young friends saw their school
buildings, the city squares and the regime's rhetoric in a
completely different light:

> The words *patria* and *Italia*, which we had found nau-
> seating within school walls because they were always
> accompanied by the adjective 'fascist', because they were
> pumped up with emptiness, suddenly appeared to us with-
> out adjectives, and so transformed that it seemed that we
> were hearing and thinking them for the first time.[2]

We can compare the two groups of youngsters, from
Turin and from Vinca. Some of the former were destined to become famous, while the latter were unknown
and partly imaginary; the former were typical children
of the twentieth century, the latter of the twenty-first.
But this comparison sparks the following burning question. How can we ensure that small groups like these
will not bend their culture and intelligence to convention and prejudice, but will instead celebrate diversity?
Will they have the necessary ability and preparedness to
connect with other, wider groups, but also with smaller
ones, mere family groups?

Paradoxically, it was easier to connect with one
another in the dramatic years of Natalia Ginzburg's
youth than in it is in our own time; for, just like the
photographs, the options of that era were expressed in
black and white. The situation under neoliberalism is
very different. Neoliberalism, the dominant ideology of
the present, is driven by consumerist passions. It projects an enfeebled imitation of democracy. It seems to
make all of us into consenting victims of its own power.
The growth of this diffuse inability to feel alternative

passions is one of the key themes in this book. Our text is motivated by a concern for politics itself; for politics' only remaining strength seems to be its power to disconnect rather than to construct shared passions that are able to react to the dissatisfaction over the present state of things. To resist *by ourselves* is no simple feat.

Despite the difficulties, we urgently need to encourage new connections and enable small, secluded groups to do more than passively submit to the choices posed by the dominant ideology. A new beginning demands new tools, because there is no point in repeating the same old rituals from the past.

This short book hopes to be such a tool. It concentrates above all on passions: not only base ones like hatred, anger and the desire to destroy whatever is different from oneself – passions so horribly unleashed in the Vinca massacre – but also higher passions, such as love, tenderness and compassion. Above all, it investigates the connection between passions and politics. It is unusual to see these two being connected – and passions and democracy even more so. But, if we question what the *emotional life of a democracy* could be, we see that a new field of reflection emerges. Of course, we do not deny that this is a complex world, but also one extremely useful to deal with – or so we hope, for all those small groups that are now growing and resolved to build something new, but not in the old way.[3]

The seductive power of neoliberal passions

Let us set our reflection within the context of the prevalent economic system of our time, namely neoliberalism. In our view, it cannot be treated just as a simple economic and political ideology. Rather, we maintain that it has such reach and influence that it pervades our everyday existence, our material and cultural consumption, our passions and our choices. We hold, moreover, that a new beginning must necessarily be laid down in discontinuity with all this.

We do not want to give in to the temptation to point to neoliberalism as the cause of all evils and all the crises that are now underway. This is too complex a historical phenomenon to be simply reduced to a single mechanism of oppression. Above all, we ought not underestimate the variety of neoliberalism's expressions or reduce it to a sequence in which an essential phenomenon comes *first* and *then* all the others, as its immediate consequences. For example, for an economist it would be tempting to believe that neoliberalism is *fundamentally* a process reorganising society's economic structures and that all the other consequences – political, anthropological, social, ethical, cultural – are inevitable corollaries of this same reorganisation. Similarly, for scholars of politics, the essence of neoliberalism is to be found in the transformation of political institutions and their sovereignty and, for philosophers, in a specific model of social rationality.

These are all parts of the truth. But they are also typical – each in its own way, of course – not just of neoliberalism but all of capitalism's historical phases. It is not new for the economy to tend to swallow up all the dimensions of society, changing its structures in the direction of increasing inequality. Nor is it new for capitalism to show an always more direct intolerance of democracy. Why, then, are all these tendencies, more or less present over the history of the last two decades,

5

being realised with ruthlessness right now, without meeting obstacles or prompting too much indignation – if only in a spontaneous or, on the contrary, elitist form – and in the absence of a well-organised political and democratic front of conflict (a conflict that in fact explodes in the form of war)?

Our answer is that the factor that has contributed to this development in neoliberalism, making it an era in which capitalism advances without being held back by any politically well-organised conflict, is above all the imposition of a unique governance of the passions. Its secret, underhand weapon is the ability to reap the benefits of a slow taming of our hearts, by now inexorably attracted to neoliberal passions. It is difficult indeed to subvert a system that has so effectively perfected its self-defence mechanisms through the seductive embrace of consumption and through control over our passions. Democratic electoral contests are now unable to release us from the system's iron grip – contests organised by a handful of people, with the help of larger and larger economic resources and through a rigid control of media that are increasingly wanting in ideas and devoid of pluralism. And even the politicians who come forth with the best of intentions end up being knocked back to the place they came from.

It is at this basic level that neoliberal government uses our passions. After all, we don't choose our passions; nor are they rational or completely free. They are called 'passions' also because we are in some sense forced to suffer* them. We might ask why most people accept policies that they would have collectively rejected once;

---

* In Italian both the verb *patire* ('endure, suffer') and the noun *passione*

why they think that the restriction of a good part of their own rights is something necessary or that it is natural to introduce a principle of competition even into the spaces inhabited by our children. And one uncomfortable but sincere answer could be: because we *want* to compete, we *want* to get rich, we *want* to become entrepreneurs of our own selves. The relationship between control over passions and neutralisation of politics in the neoliberal era helps to draw attention to an evident and decisive fact: 'neoliberalism' does not simply describe an era of history, an imbalance of the political order, an unequal recomposition of the economic classes. Its specificity also involves a form of governance over our private lives. It thus transgresses our habit of still ordering the discourse according to ancient dualisms of public–private, social–political, and so on.

This is one of neoliberalism's most powerful and most underhand weapons. It is a sort of 'Trojan horse' that insinuates itself even inside our attempts to mount a political opposition to the present system of domination. The fact that it has changed our private lives by politically reshaping the objective conditions of our existence – our education, our working life, our sphere of consumption – has also had obvious consequences for the prevalent political expectations and behaviours. It is as if all this had imposed a hegemonic ethics in which certain passions prevail over others. The way in which we engage in politics, become enthused over it or lose confidence in it seems to correspond to this hegemonic model. If even our political language and behaviour

('passion') derive from the same etymon – the Latin *patior, pati, passus sum* ('bear, undergo, suffer').

– and the common decisions that can result from them – are conditioned by passions whose driving force is not subjected to a regime of critique or consciousness, or even simply care, it will be very tough to develop political responses able to cope with the historical challenge of neoliberalism.

Moreover, this is a bitter experience, common to many people who have engaged in politics in recent years. How many attempts at building collective subjects have been foiled by some vice of passion, by an excess of selfishness or arrogance? Far more than in the case of idealistic motivations, the lack of success of these ones is much more often caused by competition among prima donnas, by an identification with the leader that ends up in a kind of voluntary servitude, by a struggle whose goal is the inflation of one's own vanity and power, by a sly diffidence displayed even towards one's own comrades, which often eventually transforms the agreement we need into mere antipathy. It is as if we sought to challenge the neoliberal order by deploying its own most effective weapons.

Here we want to point out briefly some of the elements that make up the backbone of our argument and proposals. Obviously the dominant subject here is passions. Historically, the sphere of rationality and the sphere of passions have always been separate: the triumph of reason against the weakness of sentiment, *raison d'état* against political romanticism, responsible male wisdom against female irrationality. We refuse to believe that a politics' effectiveness is directly proportional to its being immune to passions. Some justify the bid to shake off the effects of our passions on politics by invoking the latter's necessary realism; but we believe that this move has fed an underestimation of the sly governance of the passions that has imposed itself with consumer capitalism, whose fruits neoliberalism harvests. As we shall show over the next few pages, in the face of neoliberal romanticism, political realism is a blunt weapon. This is why we urgently need to try to understand our own passions, so that we can work together. We need to catalogue our passions (without falling into a sterile ennumeration of them) and to identify the ones that offer the maximum potential for democracy. As we do so, we should fight the entrenched tendency to leave the field unexplored. And we should not forget two things above all.

First, passions are always ambiguous. Even positive ones – compassion, inclusion, love – are capable of trickery and chicanery. As we shall see, precisely what characterises the present model is an *ideological* use of positive passions. They mostly serve to sweeten the pill of the brutal effects of economic and political decisions that concern our everyday lives. Their use serves not to strengthen the spaces of political critique but to anaesthetise them.

Secondly, the real difference between a critical and an ideological use of passions in the political sphere lies not so much in the distinction between positive or negative, happy or sad passions as in the distinction between passions that push towards a purely individual satisfaction and passions whose goal is the desire to build connections – that is, in the distinction *between passions without connection and shared passions*. The point of this book is not to idealise the passions. Rather we need to imagine how passions could be governed politically, with a view to uniting what, in the contemporary era, is instead constantly separated. We can also read the crisis of politics in these terms. There is almost a prohibition against common passions, which leaves us structurally incapable of elevating our individual malaise to the rank of political conflict – of transforming our legitimate need for individual recognition into a desire shared by all.

If our enquiry concentrates above all on the nature and use of passions in the political field, the second subject of constant reflection throughout this book is the state of democracy. Its multiple deficiencies in an age of grave crisis such as the one we live today are a common problem. In our view, the rebirth of democracy is necessarily linked to its capacity to develop a new affectivity and new passions.

Our goal is to help to redefine modern democratic politics. We intend to do this not only by analysing the historically given separation between the political space and the space of political virtues, but also by taking into consideration new aspects and new scenarios, which are normally detached from democratic debate. We want to demonstrate that democracy, as it is exercised today (through a representative system that has come under suspicion and that is characterised by serious imbalances and iniquities), is dragging politics into discredit; and that working on the contamination of our passions by neoliberalism can contribute (or so we intend) to strengthening the hope in collective groups that should be credible enough to set up at last a dam against the present drift. Our intention is not, then, to limit ourselves to pointing out for the umpteenth time how powerful the destructive charge of neoliberalism really is. Rather, we want to find our way back to a wellspring of affects that is still based on democratic culture and is able to oppose neoliberalism in a positive manner.

We want to respond to the following questions: How decisive is the development of an emotional wisdom to the quality of our political engagement? Which passions can obstruct a political project from turning out well, and which ones can help it succeed? These questions are not just a stylistic exercise; they are fundamental, if we are finally going to be able to set credible political processes in motion again.

One often ignored sphere in which the tension between passions and politics plays out is the family. As we shall see, it is far from being the case that love for one's family goes hand in hand with political virtues. If we are going to rethink the usefulness of the passions, both for public life and for our private lives, we need to unravel the key problem of the connection (or lack of it) between the family and the democratic state.

We realise how complex these questions are and make no pretence to be doing more than to draw attention to them. As Adorno suggests, reflection on the political organisation of the world is today closely bound up with a greater awareness of our own moral sphere: of the passions, the values, the behaviours that we choose or reject.[4]

Could it be that neoliberal *men* and *women* have the cultural and emotional formation to be able to oppose neoliberal *policies*? We think not.

1

The Debate on Passions

The ancient history of passions

Until today the term 'passions' has been used in a generic sense. We might say that passions were defined on the basis of their supposed opposite, reason. Now it is time to identify them with greater precision and trace their individual development in terms of meaning and use, especially if we want to find out how they can positively influence modern politics. Clearly, we cannot hope to cover exhaustively a theme of such long historical tradition or aspire to provide a complete typology of passions. Our aim is rather to construct an analytical method that may contribute to reinstating the passions at the centre of the political sphere.

Faced with such a difficult task, we may perhaps be forgiven for intoning the refrain of an old Beatles song: 'All you need is love, love, love'. Without doubt we need love; but love is not enough by itself, nor is it free of ambiguities, as we shall see.

When we start to list the main denominators of our

field of inquiry, we immediately realise that this is in fact a minefield. 'Passions', 'emotions', 'affects', 'feelings' and 'desires' are all terms used at a time when philosophers and political scientists have conducted intense debates, without, however, producing any consensus on their usage and meaning. Taking this into consideration, we have adopted an eclectic approach, preferring to use the terms 'passions' and 'emotions' interchangeably and sometimes opting for 'affects', though on each occasion we take care to highlight the differences of meaning and context.[1]

Both in antiquity and in the middle ages, philosophers' and thinkers' definition of the passions proceeded by way of a fundamental series of opposites. Affective life was represented in general as a *combination of positive and negative passions*. In his *Rhetoric* Aristotle cited anger and gentleness, love and enmity, fear and confidence, shame and respect, kindness and unkindness, piety and contempt, envy and emulation. Cicero's list, on the other hand, is much more restricted – it contains only four fundamental passions: pain and joy, fear and desire. Augustine sided with Cicero but radically redesigned the list in a Christian key. In his *City of God* he claims that all the passions mentioned by Cicero obey a higher prototype, namely love. Desire is the love that yearns to possess the loved; joy is the love that enjoys the possession of the loved; fear is the love that rejects its opposite; pain is the love that feels hostility and opposition to one's self-realisation. Again from the Christian tradition – more precisely, from the pen of Thomas of Aquinas in his *Summa theologiae* (written between 1265 and 1274) – we get an extraordinarily systematic analysis in this regard, and indeed one with an enormous impact. In his schema, conscious activity finds its greatest expression in God, and all actions and passion are evaluated on the basis of proximity to this source. As James writes, Thomas of Aquinas' theses find their greatest expression 'in the description of fallen humanity, in the balance between the divine and the worldly, between animals and angels'.[2]

In Thomas' classification, the first great divide takes place within what he calls 'the sense appetite', divided between a *concupiscible* and an *irascible* part. The concupiscible appetite is directed at objects and objectives of easy acquisition that are sources of pleasure or pain; the irascible, at goods that are difficult to access. Each of these major groups contains specific passions, combined, according to tradition, through a contrast between good and evil. Thus the concupiscible appetite, which is not affected by any particular doubt or difficulty over the object for which it yearns, consists of six paired passions: love (*amor*) and hatred (*odium*); the more unusual pairing of desire (*desiderium*) and flight (*fuga*, or *abomination*); and, lastly, joy (*gaudium*) and sadness (*tristitia*). By contrast, the irascible appetite – which is directed at more difficult objectives and forced to confront multiple obstacles – is composed, with a certain asymmetry, of five passions. There are two antithetical pairings: first hope (*spes*) and desire (*desiderium*), then audacity (*audacia*) and fear (*timor*). The final, isolated irascible passion is anger (*ira*) – but it is not understood in the modern sense of this term. *Ira* breaks out when it is necessary to defend a present good; it has the flavour of the Italian Resistance. Let us again quote Natalia Ginzburg: 'We were there to defend the *patria* and the *patria* was those streets and those squares, our loved ones and our childhood, and all the people who went by.'[3]

The fact that Thomas' typology sets *ira* apart, as an isolated case, warns us of the difficulty – not to say impossibility – of pairing passions in a clear antithesis between good and evil. It also makes us aware of the different meanings that one and the same term may have depending on the author who uses it. For example, anger in the sense Seneca deploys in his *De ira* – without doubt, a treatise known to Thomas – takes a much more dramatic value:

> Whether it be according to nature will become evident if we consider man's nature, than which what is more gentle while it is in its proper condition? Yet what is more cruel than anger? What is more affectionate to others than man? Yet what is more savage against them than anger? Mankind is born for mutual assistance, anger for mutual ruin: the former loves society, the latter estrangement. The one loves to do good, the other to do harm; the one to help even strangers, the other to attack even its dearest friends. The one is ready even to sacrifice itself for the good of others, the other to plunge into peril provided it drags others with it.[4]

Hobbes, Descartes, Spinoza

How have these first distinctions and typologies evolved and changed over time? What meanings have they taken on in more recent centuries? A particularly rich debate developed in seventeenth-century Europe.[5] It was marked by the interventions of thinkers of the stature of Hobbes, Descartes and Spinoza. Except for Spinoza, who was probably the most modern-minded among them, these philosophers considered the passions to be a source of unlimited harms, just as their predecessors had. They held that passion, in sharp contrast with the pure light of reason, 'blinds' people, reducing them to wayfarers cut adrift in the mist after having lost their bearings. It is a familiar argument: the philosophers of the seventeenth century attributed especially to women this peculiar incapacity to put the brakes on their passions and to think rationally. Hence the need to confine them to the domestic and reproductive sphere.

This generalised fear in the face of passions demanded that various strategies be thought up in order to contain them. The relationship between passions and politics, too, remained trapped inside this assumption, as Hobbes and Descartes show in exemplary fashion.

In Hobbes we find a reduction of passions to their elements. There is no need to waste time listing them or distinguishing the terms, nor is there too much difference between them: all passions are quantitative variations of *conatus essendi*, our desire to exist. What does 'quantitative variations' mean? That the passions are always sensations: they concern the body.

This elementary materialism of the passions has a valuable consequence for our own discourse: it reduces any attempt to reflect on passions or to govern them to a merely private feat. Each person has her own passions and reconstructs, evaluates, feels and projects these passions over time on the basis of her own imagination or memory.[6] Similar passions can be governed in different ways, on the basis of each person's specific traits. If we were not forced to articulate our passions together with our needs, these infinite hues in the modes of interpreting our passions would surely be no problem. Unfortunately, however, at the very moment in which each person discovers that she cannot do without meeting other human beings along her own path, this extremely simple autonomy in governing one's own passions becomes a menace. It is at this point that Hobbes, in spite of himself, does take up a list of passions, indicating which ones should be at the base of our social relations: 'First, Competition; Secondly, Diffidence; Thirdly, Glory.'[7] How relevant does this list of passions appear today, if we compare it with the passions that we now consider it natural to use in our political relations? Let's try to summarise. For Hobbes passions are not, in themselves, an object of inner discernment or moral judgement: we need not discuss them, still less write a little book like our own. They are sensations, perceived in peaceable fashion by the matter of which we are made. However, as soon as we enter into society this proprietary, peaceful individualism transforms itself into a competitive individualism. I can no longer treat passions in the same way as I do some object I possess; I am no longer free to do what I want with it. Certain passions no longer bring us peace but drive us to war. Curiously, Hobbes defines the difference between humans and animals precisely starting from these passions. He asks himself why animals don't go to war: because their passions remain exclusively confined to individual satisfaction (perhaps Hobbes did not see enough of the interminable mimetic fights that drive the rivalry among the cats in our gardens). Forced to compete with others, the human being feels that wholly human sensation that Hobbes himself labels 'anxiety'. Hobbes thus offers a description of this emotional state that remains highly relevant today. As a sort of perennial experience of low-intensity warfare, anxiety is an exclusively *human* passion.

If, in individual life, every passion descends from our desires, in social life it is envy that takes the place of desire. And it is at this point that passions – the unpolitical matter par excellence, because they are tied to the individual – do legitimise politics. No person involved in social competition can govern her own passions with fairness.

Hobbes thus provides an interpretation of the relationship between passions and politics (more precisely, between a theory of affects and a theory of power) that still conditions our common experience. He suggests, above all, that the natural sphere of passions be limited to a simple, private affair. He then defines, indirectly, the passions that colonise our social and political relations and that have to do exclusively with the figure of the envious man. Envy – this irresistible passion that transforms social relations into opportunities for competition, diffidence, honour – can be limited not by rationality, but by force. The force of the sovereign – the one who does not use passions and is a guarantor for all – is legitimised by the impossibility of finding a solution autonomously and of limiting the irrepressibility of passions. *The envious man ends up changing into a subjected man.*

In this, the politician's role is that of the person who controls our passions but is not controlled by them. The politician is legitimised by them, but is also able to take a distance from them. We could also put it this way: her political capacity is certainly not influenced by her way of governing her passions – which ones she habitually dominates and which ones she habitually uses. Her capacity consists exclusively of her force. If a politician is strong, in other words able to subject the passions of others and thus to keep at bay the unpleasant consequences that are always lurking, then it is utterly indifferent whether that politician is cruel or benevolent, timorous or confident. Passions remain in the backdrop of political life, as a characteristic of the subject. They do so as an object of politics' own concern, not as an intrinsic element that contributes to determining its own forms and processes.

In other authors, instead, an intense fear of passions was often accompanied by strenuous efforts to limit their field of operation. Both Descartes and Spinoza warned of the need to introduce a distinction between passions and emotions. They assigned emotions the role of limiting the dangerous influence of passions. Both philosophers attached a qualifying adjective to the term 'emotions'.

For Descartes, '*inner* emotions' are drives awakened by the soul itself, and not – like passions – awakened by the 'animal spirit' or by physical reactions, which are merely bodily. Inner emotions come into play at the moment when a person pursues virtue with the force of will and the power of reason. The effort to make virtue prevail is heavily compensated for at the emotional level. For the happiness that derives from virtue is a potent antidote against the threats that the passions raise to the soul's serenity.

Descartes treats the relationship between inner emotions and passions in the manner of a constant struggle between wholly separate and antithetical forces. The tranquillity of the soul – which positively resolves this battle – plays the same function that Hobbes ascribed the sovereign. If in Hobbes politics was not dominated by passions but rather dominated them, as a sort of external constraint, here there is no need for any external control. Passions, which belong to the ego, are dominated by the ego.

Descartes suggests, therefore, that from a certain point of view there could be a sort of self-government of the passions before there is any political involvement, whereas Hobbes requires a political labour on passions to pre-empt the disaster to which individual passions would lead us, once they have been abandoned to social competition.

The soul's capacity to distinguish clearly between 'inner emotions' and 'false passions' is proper not to the *envious person*, but rather to what we may call a *generous person*. Generosity is the virtue of the person who adapts her own passions to what can reasonably be done.[8] Descartes' position – seen with today's eyes – suffers from at least two limitations.

The first of these is his own incorrigible dualism, for which the passions of the ego are in reality the passions of the ego's rationality. Even though they also indirectly concern *res extensa* (that is, the body), they remain something ethereal and unembodied, vulnerable to rational control. They are *passions without bodies*.

The second limitation is that the passions controlled by the soul end up being resolved in an experience wholly disconnected from other human beings. There remain only *passions without ties*. Which, projected onto the contours of the relationship between passions and politics, is decidedly symptomatic.

The Cartesian is generous, yes, but only towards

herself (and, even then, not in a complete way but in ignorance of the passions of the body). The discernment of 'inner emotions' is limited to our private space, which must be protected from any political interference. Descartes' suggestion risks being truly unsparing. In certain respects it resembles that bitter disenchantment with the help of which a lot of people keep any temptation of political involvement at bay. Better to concentrate all our strength on seeking to live virtuously, holding politics as far off as possible; after all, politics destabilises us, corrupts us, forces us in a position where we can't handle passions as we should. Either we chose to be virtuous people or we choose to be strong politicians.

There is a suspicion about the political sphere, and it is spreading: it always lies in ambush, ready to threaten our capacity to govern passions rightfully. We can govern them only so long as we do not provoke the force of the power external to us. Certainly, Descartes had good historical reasons to argue all of this. But we are not conditioned by the same history that troubled Descartes, even if our history is itself anything but peaceful (as the cemetery at Vinca teaches us). So why is it still so widely believed that the political dimension not only does not help our capacity to regulate our passions and live virtuously, but disturbs it? That we need a 'minimal state', precisely in order to limit the potential conflicts so destructive to our already precarious individual balance? The person who is generous to himself also proves to be a person obedient to power. She is well aware that having too many attachments (and too much political involvement) is a threat to success in handling our inner emotions.

Spinoza's strength consists precisely in the fact that, within the game of passions, he values these two sources that are lost in Descartes: the *body* and *attachments*. His '*intellectual* emotions' are also driven by reason but, unlike Descartes' 'inner emotions', they are not located exclusively within the soul. For Spinoza, intellectual emotions, just like passions, are the product of both the body and the mind. The difference lies in their content and their character, not in their location on one side or another of the body–mind border. Put simply, for Spinoza inadequate ideas stir passions and adequate ideas give rise to intellectual emotions. Yet this distinction should not at all be understood in a dualistic sense, and hence as an underestimation of the body's role in our experience of passions. Intellectual emotions are the fruit of a wisdom that traverses the body. We can know, feel and measure our passions and emotions. But what makes us able to measure them is certainly not the autonomy of reason from the body.

For Spinoza there is no wisdom that does not come from the body. This is why whatever we can know of our emotions comes from our body. In a stroke, the body takes centre stage when it comes to passions and, at the same time, becomes the fundamental subject of their governing.[9] It is always possible for us to err in our passions (above all, in relation to some defect of the imagination), but this is not at all inevitable. The deeper our knowledge of the passions, the more we can elevate them and use them for the best. And, to know our passions well, we must first of all take our bodies seriously. The essential criterion for this knowledge comes – according to Spinoza – from the famous distinction between sad passions and joyous ones. Sad passions are those in which we feel some frustration or diminution of our *desire*, of our *active* possibilities. We feel that we are passing from a state of greater perfection to one of lesser perfection. Joyous passions, on the contrary, are those in which our desire to be is amplified and we feel that we are heading towards a state of greater perfection. This distinction between sad passions and joyous ones will be fundamental to our proposal. First of all, one should take care not to interpret this distinction erroneously, as an umpteenth list of good passions and wicked ones. Indeed, joyous passions are not necessarily positive passions (and vice versa). The things that bring about some increase in our perfection and in our desire do not always follow peaceful routes. This strange wisdom redefines the contours of certain passions' political values in the following way: it suggests that passions like love or benevolence can be sad ones, if they do not serve to augment the value of our existence, and that, on the contrary, passions like indignation in the face of injustice, or rage, can be joyous when they serve to exercise a conflict able to change the current state of things.

To conclude: the first indication that we can draw from Spinoza is that, if we are looking for a way to govern passions, we need not put them in chains, disembodying them or subjecting them to the rigid control of some other, more reliable faculty (which could be rationality but, just as often, is a preventative adherence to some religious or moral model – one that prescribes which passions are more advantageous and which are less so). We may think that the governing of passions is a human practice wholly immanent in our nature (or substance). Spinoza suggests that there can be a reliable and non-despotic way of governing one's own passions that does not necessarily mean repressing or sublimating them. The human being does not simply have passions happen to her, but can flourish and draw benefit from them (the *passions* that are not simply happenings are none other than the *affects*).

The second suggestion refers specifically to the connection between passions and politics. Particularly in his incomplete *Tractatus politicus*, Spinoza tried to show how the wisdom that we can achieve by governing the passions is essentially political in nature. For politics is the place where we can experience a strange type of passions: the 'common passions'.[10] And what is the force of these passions? It resides in the fact that we can experience even more joyous passions and attain states of always greater perfection only through the potential of our coming together. Attachments are not the enemy of a good government of passions but represent its principal ally. The political regime in which this greater perfection can be achieved in an extended, horizontal form – without domination, violence or other sad passions – could be democracy itself.

Spinoza died before finishing this first part of his *Tractatus politicus*. Nonetheless, despite its incompleteness, his provocation is completely fascinating. It is not only that politics does not have to mistrust the passions or simply use them as a weapon of cultural, communicative and political domination. Rather politics defines itself through its capacity to reinforce our passions, to make them even stronger, even more liberating, even more authentic. This is a true and proper political governance of the passions. Only this political governance is not transcendent, superior or external. As we say in such cases, it is immanent: it coincides with the passions themselves, which get expanded, become interlinked, are understood through intellectual labour, and clash in a naturally extensive and political form. The resurgence of Spinoza's concept of the 'power of one multitude' is one of the most significant tendencies in the reflection on politics during recent decades.

Certainly, in view of our own experience, this seems completely dated. There are at least two objections that need answering. What happens when democracy is far from being the place where joyous passions manifest themselves, and is instead one where sad passions predominate? And, on the other hand, what happens when politics uses the joyous passions offered by neoliberalism to conceal our perfection and make us feel worse? Perhaps we should use Spinoza to insist, loudly, that the trajectories of our political relations and the spaces in which they operate need to be rethought, and that this starts with a construction of the passions that is truly and properly common. Again, we are betting on the fact that the true force of politics – the thing that still determines its fascination, despite everything – is not domination, but rather its capacity to allow us unprecedented satisfactions and passions that we can share with others. Without this common construction – so the philosopher seems to be telling us – politics loses any sense of wisdom and turns into domination.

This analysis of the passions cannot do without considering another great cultural movement, namely romanticism. Rather than put a brake or a yoke on the passions or deprive them of their drama, romanticism places them at the centre of its extraordinary universe. Politically, this was a motley, even contradictory movement, though one based on the conviction that modern society will be doomed if it proves unable to express 'the true essence of reality'. For example, the exponents of early German romanticism were under the impression that they were living a threefold alienation: from their own selves, from their neighbour and from nature. Seeking to do justice (at least in part) to romanticism, we have chosen to devote a specific section to it (see pp. 39–60). This allows us to compare the liberal romanticism of the first half of the nineteenth century with its neoliberal counterpart, transforming its dark Gothic cathedrals into neon-lit hypermarkets.[11]

Passions' active function: Feminism

Before moving on to the comparison between political and neoliberal romanticism, we should declare our debt to the tradition of thought that has revealed, more than any other, politics' structural diffidence vis-à-vis the passions. This critical distance from that modern attitude is in fact an indisputable, historic merit of feminism. Feminism does not represent one stage among the others in the long and intricate history that serves to define the relations between passion and politics. It represents something much more profound: a critical point of view that asks us to call into question the traditional way in which we write (and read) that history. We need only recall Pateman's famous thesis that it is the social contract itself – the consolidated form of our political relations – that is founded on subordination to the male order and is a real sexual contract.[12]

The risk today is that we end up accepting that 'feminist theory is nothing more than the inclusion of women and the relation between the sexes into existing theories'.[13] We should have by now enough of a sensitivity to refuse to participate in a political space where sex difference is reduced to an insignificant factor (or just one among others). Unfortunately, reality seems to fall short of such expectations. Hence we need to persevere along the path of a true critical rewriting of the relationship between passions and politics. It is entirely clear that the questions we would like to put back at the centre of the discussion in these pages are the bequest of the rewriting operated by feminism. In particular, we want to retrieve some of its arguments that are more relevant now than ever.

The first argument is that, within the political sphere, there is an analogy between the process by which passions are subordinated and the process by which women are subordinated. As Sara Ahmed reminds us,

> Emotions are associated with women, who are represented as 'closer' to nature, ruled by appetite, and less able to transcend the body through thought, will and judgement.[14]

On what scaffolding, then, is this twofold subordination of women and of passions built? On the naturalisation of the relationship between them. It is natural that women are dominated by certain passions, just as it is natural that men can transcend them through their grip on rationality. Passions (*some* passions) would, then, be nothing more than the inheritance of an anti-modern time, almost a residue deposited in women's bodies through some oversight of evolutionary history (a little like men's body hair!). The naturalisation of the relationship between passions and gender is a murderous weapon, because it does not allow us any margins for working on passions or for governing them.

In helping to pull apart this knot, feminism has proposed a truly revolutionary critical paradigm: passions are cultural, relational and historically founded. None of us simply suffers them, and none of us is constrained by them as if by nature. Passions act and produce our actions and our choices, and in so doing contribute to the processes of recognition and of the attribution of meaning. They are made of language, bodies, relations, histories. Above all, they are made of conflicts, the most vivid example of the extent to which passions condition political histories. In fact, it is the passions we invest in conflicts that decide whether the latter will appear in a violent form or in a properly political form, as conflicts founded on personalisation and narcissism or as conflicts founded on shared passions. Indeed, one of this book's fundamental theses is the following: the undiscussed, unanimous acceptance of neoliberal passions allows contemporary politics to privilege in a peaceful manner the staging of conflicts of this first type – gigantic contests based on the recurrent representation of the strength of one leader against another – and to suffocate any authentically political conflict – that is, any hard-fought and non-violent debate that seeks to contribute to our shared deliberation on how society should be governed.

A politics of passions proceeds by eliminating the naturalisation of passions in favour of privileging their performativity, their capacity to produce, in unexpected fashion, relations and languages, behaviours and meanings, thereby investing them with the responsibility to conduct a careful choice of the combinations of passions and states of mind that will act as an incentive to a radically different politics.

Passions' active function: Feminism

Our second thesis, then, is that it is worth trying to start out once more from this active function of passions, in order to reactivate the civic value of politics; and to do so by displacing a still too entrenched *forma mentis* that has put passions out of place, arranged according to predetermined spaces and subjects. This is well described in the following passage:

We could say, in a word, that men become bearers of public passions (heroism, courage in war, the brotherhood of the sect, the passion for politics and, last but not least, the passion for power) ... Women, for their part, become the architects par excellence of private sentiments, confined to the family and the domestic environment.[15]

How can we deactivate this entrenched attitude, in which certain subjects are deputised to politics while others are condemned to the domestic sphere? Feminism suggests *two overlapping ways forward*. As we shall see in the following pages, in both cases the important thing is to insist on the need to carry out a kind of sidestep with respect to representative democracy.

The *first way* invites us to imagine political spaces as sites in which identities, histories, relations and languages are produced, and not only as spaces for the production of power. It is probably no longer sufficient to be nostalgic about politics as the chosen space of power (and its passions), notwithstanding the gloomy, urgent feeling that now permanently weighs down on us. Perhaps it is time to embrace the critique of power – of power *as* passion, of the male character has accompanied it, hand in hand, over the centuries, selecting public passions and private feelings – to embrace it, that is, as an opportunity to make politics into a site where we become people and build communities, and not only where we decide on other people's behalf (most often against them).

In short, feminism helps us to ask again the question that rests at the very origin of the interweaving between passions and politics. It asks us not simply 'What *are* the passions?' but, most importantly, 'What do the passions *do*?' It gets us absorbed into how passions make us into active *subjects* of politics through that strange interweaving of social and individual elements, to which they belong.

This move is accompanied by a *second, apparently opposite way* – the one indicated by feminism's historic teaching that the personal is political. Even today, this is a genuine programme of political action. If a spell of depoliticisation has cancelled out any attraction to political engagement, we can, however, seek to repoliticise our everyday lives: to resist in our emotional life, to experiment familial spaces able to safeguard new and politically edifying passions, to oppose the disenchantment of precarious lives with new representations of labour as a form of life in common. Above all, to discover that the passions that walk around with us also define our political preferences and behaviours.

At last – and this is the third thesis – feminism with its embrace of conflict helps us to grasp that the political diffidence vis-à-vis passions arises from an impulse as understandable as it is ugly. For, as we have just written, passions produce conflicts and are not easily commanded or controlled. They do not produce unanimous agreement or an easy consensus. They call for a common deliberation on how they should be governed. The feeling that recurs most often is that the still prevalent male politics has restricted us to spheres in which we are no longer able to distinguish between 'waging a war' and 'living through a conflict'. The ethics of conflict demands the recognition that differences can never be cancelled out entirely and that, as Arendt warned, a uniformisation of passions will produce a petrified society.[16] Remaining within the conflict means together seeking out a constructive government of passions, connecting different passions, states of mind and attitudes – such as gentleness and steadfastness – and finding a way to manage the discord in a virtuous form. What we urgently need is a political ecology of passions.

Governing and combining passions

Aided by authoritative past reflection, we have sought to shed light on some fundamental indicators that can help us to arrive at an innovative conjugation of the relationship between the exercise of politics and the government of passions.

At first sight, the typologies identified in antiquity and in the middle ages seem to promise a simple solution. Extrapolating the positive passions from Aristotle, Cicero and Thomas' respective pairs of opposites, we get a long list: love, kindness, piety, gentleness, joy, hope, trust, respect, desire, emulation, audacity, and even anger (in Thomas' sense). We can discuss the ranking of these positive passions as much as we like, but could we not simply bunch them together and enrol them in the fight for an 'impassioned politics'? The answer is yes, though with some considerable reservations. Things are a lot more complicated, and we should proceed by elaborating a series of qualifications and limits.

The first is that passions can change, at both the

individual or historical level. All too often, we are individually forced to admit that a passion has an intrinsic ambivalence that can easily transform it into something negative: love into hate, compassion into indifference, desire into disgust. Shakespeare provided unparalleled evidence of this in *Hamlet*:

> The violence of either grief or joy
> Their own enactures with themselves destroy.
> Where joy most revels grief doth most lament;
> Grief joys, joy grieves, on slender accident.[17]

To put it simply, positive passions are not so easily identifiable, or available, or necessarily constant. In historical terms, we should recognise that, over time, both positive and negative passions vary in importance. Some disappear while others gain a weight they never had in the era of Descartes and Spinoza. In her essay *Emotions in History*, Ute Frevert follows the developments of *akēdia* [ἀκηδία, 'indifference, apathy']. In ancient Greek, the term designated a sort of apathy. Thomas Aquinas defined it as 'the pain of the world', while in English it can be translated 'sloth' and in German *Trägheit* ['sloth, indolence']. Over time, *akēdia* disappeared and became a 'lost emotion', replaced by the term 'depression' in its modern use – a term that appears for the first time in the psychological lexicon in 1905 and has enjoyed an extraordinary diffusion ever since.[18] Less widely used, but more pertinent to modern politics is the term 'narcissism'. It has a long history and, as we shall see, strong connections with contemporary neoliberal romanticism. Negative passions that have disappeared from the lexicon have often been replaced by new ones. Anxiety is a good example. Negative passions make for bigger subjects of analysis and debate because they are medicalised – something that does not happen with positive passions. As a discipline and as an industry, psychoanalysis makes negative passions its very foundation. But no one invests time and money to analyse purely positive emotions. Who would visit a psychoanalyst because he is happy?

In some cases old and new emotions coincide, even if they are endowed with specific meanings that differ. Thus Aristotle's 'mildness' is similar to our own 'gentleness', which has considerably come back in fashion in recent times. Generally, however, the set of positive political passions today would have to be strongly differentiated from the traditional ones analysed in the past. On a contemporary list, next to love we would surely find love for peace, compassion, generosity, sympathy, and something that might be called ecoempathy, or more simply respect for the natural world. Making these passions the foundation of emotional life in a new republic would itself be an extraordinary result. But this is not sufficient and could even be misleading.

Some passions that are positive on the terrain of interpersonal relations may not be at all positive when it comes to the political sphere: love can be good for justice, but justice certainly cannot end up being identified with love. Any absolutisation of a passion makes it politically useless in the end. Just as a politics that cuts out positive passions and privileges negative ones (cynicism, ambition, hostility, hatred) in absolute fashion will finally exclude a considerable share of legitimate human aspirations, a politics exclusively founded on positive passions will prove unable to be concrete and equitable and will risk resembling an 'empire of the good'.

More generally, we think that any *despotic* government

of passions – in which there is a sort of primacy of some passions over others – should be abandoned. Rather than set them hierarchically, we need to recover a polyphony of passions. To envisage, also on the political terrain, a constant articulation of passions with other passions or behaviours and states of mind, which can in some sense determine their use and intention.

A passage in Thomas Aquinas seems to anticipate this suggestion. Passions should be governed 'not by a "despotic supremacy", which is that of a master over his slave; but by a "politic and royal supremacy", whereby the free are governed, who are not wholly subject to command'.[19] Isolated passions, or ones left to themselves – even positive ones – are particularly vulnerable politically. It is necessary to create an environment and a context in which they can survive and prosper, a virtuous circle similar to the one established in a gift culture, where each person gives and receives. This effort not to leave passions isolated can be highly productive. Let us propose a series of combinations, without presuming that the list is complete.

First of all, a political government of passions demands that they be always contextualised and, even more radically, that the use of passions always pay heed to the contexts in which it is exercised. There are passions that belong to the discursive regime specific to small groups and that could not turn useful in wider contexts (to give just one example, the use of anger bears strong traces of the contexts in which it is exercised).

Secondly, a passion can be contained or governed through its bond with an internal behaviour or state of mind. For example, hope – ever present on all the lists of passions offered by tradition – can be a politically counterproductive passion when it tends to accelerate the timescales and to force the discussion so that everyone may share in it and the positions defined may be consistent with it. In such situations, an excess of hope can be contained through combination with patience – which is a state of mind and not another passion.

Lastly, the risk of absolutising a passion can be avoided by structurally pairing it with another passion. The best example is the political passion par excellence: ambition – or vanity. It is ingrained in the politician's personality. But if it is not to become destructive it must be flanked by other, less self-centred passions: the passion for an ideal, or temperance.

These three examples – the evaluation of passions within specific contexts, their combination with states of mind or elements of behaviour, and their pairing with other passions – show that, in contemporary politics, a governance over the passions can be effective only if it is not reduced to a rivalry between more or less noble and positive passions, each standing in isolation from another. Methodologically, this demands a care and a prior agreement that should allow all those who want to engage in politics to be able to share an 'alphabet of passions' that makes them feel reassured and welcome and opens the way to the chance of an otherwise impossible political creativity.

Another example of the need to combine the passions is gentleness. When Norberto Bobbio's famous article 'In Praise of Meekness' was published in 1994, a debate developed around the potential and practical validity of this passion.[20] It is immediately worth noting that, when Bobbio addressed gentleness, he did not use the vocabulary of passions and emotions but rather considered gentleness a virtue. What may seem a point-less complication in our discourse could serve instead to shed light on one of its essential traits. Without discussing the merit of a problem that has occupied scores of philosophers, we could in fact ask the following question: What marks the difference between a passion and a virtue, in the area of our political behaviour? We could say that virtues are ways of deploying passions in a stable form. Our use of the passions becomes virtuous when it helps to define a prevalent form of life for each person: a form of life that is enduring and publicly recognisable.

For this reason the politician should be neither without passions nor enslaved to her own passions. She makes passions part of a permanent exercise of caring about her own words and actions. This means a constant exercise of self-government, which is not simply a matter of relations with others. The politician is not supposed to put her own passions on display, but to make them serve her political tasks and responsibilities. Any political education is also a sentimental one. The virtuous politician is the one who is able to govern her own passions without either using them up or letting herself be dominated by them. In this way, through her behaviour, the politician makes herself worthy of the authority incumbent upon her. We will see as much in chapter 3.

For Bobbio, this relationship between virtue and power, which defines the personality of the politician, is precisely what makes gentleness a controversial virtue. It is a weak virtue, not a strong one, in the sense that it belongs to that component of society that does not exercise power: the 'humiliated and the insulted, the subjects who will never be sovereigns'.[21] Then again, gentleness is something quite different from submission. It is a *social* virtue, a serene but different vision of the world: 'a meek person is someone needed by others to help them defeat the evil within themselves', writes Bobbio.[22] Numerous virtues complement gentleness: simplicity and clemency, honesty and clarity, compassion.

But gentleness needs more than complementary virtues; it must be supported unconditionally by other elements, in a contest that proves to be utterly imbalanced. In other words, it needs company, especially in the world of politics. For Bobbio, whatever its advantages, gentleness is not a political virtue: 'rather it is the most impolitical of virtues'. He asks us to bear in mind that in chapter 18 of Machiavelli's *The Prince* the two animals that symbolise the politician are the lion and the wolf. There is no space, he writes, for the gentle 'sheep', which is most likely doomed to be the victim. Yet Machiavelli's vision of politics is not the only one that exists. Looking at a figure like Gandhi, we immediately see how very difficult it is to reduce him to Machiavellian categories. Despite its considerable efforts, the British imperial lion did not succeed in devouring him. In reality, Gandhi's story encourages us not to distinguish between strong and weak virtues or passions, but rather to identify a necessary combination between them that we find in Gandhi's own political biography, which united *pacifism with gentleness and steadfastness*. Today as well, gentleness and resolution are an essential combination for our idea of politics.

The history of *Volksgemeinschaft* – the 'people's community' of the Nazis from 1933 to 1945 – offers another example of the need to combine different passions.

How can we distinguish between our own civic passions and those of *Volksgemeinschaft*? This question seems easy enough to answer, but it is not. If we look into *Volksgemeinschaft*, we find many apparently 'positive' passions that we could accept without much thought. There was compassion for the German families struck by unemployment, there was very active support for the *Winterhilfswerk* (the Winter Relief Fund for the German People), there was love for the sons and soldiers killed in the First World War or in street battles against communist groups, and there was solidarity, kindness and generosity. But Nazism bound all this to an utterly ferocious set of exclusivist passions – discrimination, submission, deportation and killing. It is precisely these passions that make this example so distant from us.

Therefore, if we are to establish the distinction between the Nazi case and modern welfare democracy – between their Reich and our republic – we need to privilege a particular set of *unwavering* passions and attitudes, and indeed to make them explicit. These are inclusion, sharing, acceptance, the refusal to stigmatise the other. Only when other very widespread emotions like familial compassion, which we will look at in our last chapter, are combined with those 'inclusive' passions just listed above can they hope to bear fruit within a democratic system.

In conclusion, the hope of inventing a new democratic politics relies on different attitudes, on a more focused and conscious choice of passions, and on the relationship between passions and self-government.

2
Political Romanticism and Neoliberal Romanticism

Political romanticism

In his famous 1925 essay *Political Romanticism*,[1] Carl Schmitt argues that the romantic movement flowering in Europe at the end of the eighteenth century and in the first half of the nineteenth gave rise to a form of politics characterised by a dangerous and untrammelled supremacy of the passions. For Schmitt – one of the most famous political theorists of the twentieth century, also known for his Nazi sympathies – political romanticism was the poisonous fruit of individualism and secularism, both rooted in the French Revolution. In the absence of the ordered dictates of the church and of the state, 'it is left to the private individual to be his own priest'.[2] *Bildungsgeschichte* ('the construction of individual consciousness'), which was such an integral part of romanticism – one shared by figures as varied as Friedrich Schlegel and John Stuart Mill – was in Schmitt's eyes simply a process in which individuals substituted their own narcissism for any real contact with the modern world.

According to Schmitt, this state of affairs led the romantics to 'romanticise' reality, to 'detach' it, to fail to establish an even minimal link between cause and effect in the public sphere. In his view, the best definition that could be applied to political romanticism was that of 'subjectivised occasionalism', in other words the condition in which the individual invented reality on the strength of his own instincts and whims, imagining opportunities for them.

Any student of European nationalism in the first half of the nineteenth century or of its contemporary homologue in Latin America would have no difficulty in finding examples of the syndrome that Schmitt describes. But this discourse has a much wider sweep. The romanticism of the early nineteenth century did not have just one political expression. It was simultaneously revolutionary and counter-revolutionary, democratic and aristocratic, red and white, retrograde and utopian. But, amid all its extraordinarily richness and multiplicity, its protagonists identified a series of shared objectives that continue to be at the centre of the relationship between politics and passions today. Taken as a whole, these constitute a sort of 'civic project'.

The first objective, already mentioned briefly, is the realisation of individual freedom, understood as a cultural construction free of screens set up by the individual.

A second objective is human sympathy – like that which Wordsworth expressed in his relationship with the inhabitants of the Lake District and in his desire to live together with them in natural harmony. The same sentiment – expressed in a very different way – was also apparent in the relationship between Byron and the *car-*

bonari of Ravenna in 1820–1.[3] These were small groups of like-minded, dissenting individuals who gave rise to communities of a more or less binding character. We find various declensions of the fundamental concept of human sympathy in Burke, Novalis, Lamennais and Lamartine – other protagonists of the romantic movement.[4] Individual freedom and human sympathy are two key elements of political romanticism. A third component is love of nature and respect for it. The romantic passion for nature was not exclusively based on the admiration and fear that nature stirs in humanity, but on the damaging effect that human actions have on nature and on the need to safeguard the natural world from the onslaught of all-consuming capitalist relations. In *Lucinde*, Friedrich Schlegel writes: 'What's the point, then, of this unremitting aspiration and progress without rest and purpose?'[5] And, in his famous poem 'The world is too much with us', William Wordsworth perfectly grasped the dangers inherent in the nascent consumer society, unbound as it is by rules:

> The world is too much with us; late and soon
> Getting and spending, we lay waste our powers:
> Little we see in nature that is ours;
> We have given our hearts away, a sordid boon![6]

In this light, far from being detached from the modern world – the irredeemable dreamers portrayed by Schmitt – the romantics revealed themselves to be extraordinarily sensitive to one of the most pressing problems of modernity.

Obviously, the romantic movement was afflicted by failings and weaknesses. One of the most important can be found on the terrain of gender politics. There are few female voices within the movement, and still fewer male ones that called for women to have an equal and active role in associative life. In 1848 Clotilde Koch-Gontard, wife of a Frankfurt merchant, found it 'rather depressing to be only a woman, always the spectator of events'. In April 1848, together with a female friend, she managed secretly to enter the Paulskirche and hear the debates of the new German parliament.[7]

In the civic project of romanticism, men were normally called on to reach passionately for the sublime. This aesthetics assumed a strong gender connotation. Women, conversely, had to cultivate *beauty*, defined as delicateness, submissiveness, an angelic quality. They were ascribed the passions of the home. Disdainful of repetitive everyday routines, instead searching for brief and intense moments of passion, romantic men were not natural candidates for the roles of the good husband or father.[8]

These tendencies to a strong gender demarcation were further accentuated by the fascination that militarism and the glory of arms exercised over the romantics. Percy Shelley's pacifist positions made him an almost isolated case. The yearning to follow the great romantic military leaders – Napoleon first among them – and to be ready for the sublime action of sacrificing one's own life are hyper-recurrent themes, themselves linked to the nationalist and religious fanaticism that would exercise such a sinister influence on the entire modern world. For all its limits, the liberal tradition held firm against this fanaticism. John Stuart Mill was not the only one to despise republicanism's militarist tradition, preferring to it the commercial society based on the values of comfort, security and personal freedom.[9]

Political romanticism

We can identify one last field, full of tragic shadows and a few rare sparks of resplendent light, in what was perhaps the greatest passion of all: romantic love. *Amour passion* was a matter of elective affinities, of reaching otherness for a moment, of the ecstatic discovery of the lips and sometimes of the body of another. But perhaps it was above all a sickness. Leopardi, who had a perfect understanding of this field, described its symptoms as 'that worry and that desire and that discontent and that mania and that distress that come with strength of passion'.[10] Romantic love was rarely satisfied and shared in totality. At least in the literature of the time, it was often *impossible*, for if it did concede a momentary approach to the sublime it condemned the sick man or woman to long periods of suffering and desperation. We will soon see how this rebel passion would be materialised and quenched by neoliberalism's (obligatory) offer of consumption.

Nonetheless, in romanticism's civic project and in its highest cultural and political expressions, we can make out a highly important combination, which associates passion with discipline. Identified *in primis* by Isaiah Berlin, this is another example of the combinations we described in the previous chapter. The great romantic successes were never exclusively based on inspiration and passion; rather they were grounded in the subjection of emotions and visions to a rigid discipline, which aimed to give them appropriate form. 'Hot' and 'cold', passion and rationality, had to be combined. This concept will remain a continuing presence throughout the rest of this book. As Isaiah Berlin puts it, Schubert said 'that the mark of a great composer is to be caught in a vast battle of inspiration, in which the forces rage in the most uncontrolled way, but to keep one's head in the course of the storm and direct the troops'.[11] To a certain extent this marriage of passion and discipline led to the extraordinary success of Garibaldi's expedition to Sicily in May 1860. We are certainly very far here from Carl Schmitt's disdainful judgement and complete repudiation of romanticism.

Political romanticism thus appears in a more complex light. Not all the passions it evokes and (in some cases) creates are welcome and useful. The excesses of *amour passion*, the 'sublime' sentiments awakened not only by nature but also by the experiences of war, and the movement's total lack of sensitivity to matters of gender are all elements that undermine any attempt to establish connections between passions and present-day politics. But other elements – individual freedom, cultural creativity (the 1815–48 period remains without equal on this terrain), the love of nature and hatred of industrialism, the sympathy frequently expressed towards other human beings and animals – are a truly precious legacy. The passion associated with self-government (and discipline) can produce rather surprising results.[12]

Consumer capitalism and neoliberal romanticism

In a recent volume that significantly brought the connection between political life and emotions back to the centre of the more general public debate, Martha Nussbaum warns us about what she defines as a genuine 'problem in the history of liberalism'.[13] For Nussbaum, this problem consists of the paradox that the capacity to orient public emotions is considered one of the strong points of the most prominent politicians, and yet the role of the emotions is not itself deemed important enough to be a specific object of reflection on political forms.[14] We ought to recognise that this oversight applies not only to intellectuals but also to both political and civil society (perhaps *especially* to the latter). The persuasion that taking greater care of the qualities of the emotions activated in the public space is one of our 'civic' responsibilities does not seem to have become widespread.

We could summarise this problem as follows: we underestimate the public function of emotions even though we admit that today a significant part of political power is exercised on this very terrain. The result is that we witness an ever greater political use of emotions (we need only think of the representation of terrorism and of migration movements) and, on the other hand, we persist in the belief that, while political emotions are important, they do not require too much attention and should not be studied or directed.

But Nussbaum's thesis has a theoretical limit: what an intellectual sees as a *problem*, a political activist simply sees as a *resource*.

One political category that demonstrates to perfection this inversion is the category of the leader. What is the leader – at least as we see things in the western democracies – if not a politician who shifts public opinion simply by using the charismatic force of emotions and empathy? These leader democracies take root in a political neoromanticism. In an age of post-democracies, the acceptance of the need for a leader seems to be one of those bipartisan dogmas. Of course, the models we could take as examples are varied: from fascination with the commander-in-chief typical of western political history to fascination with the direct link between leader and people in the Latin American tradition. But in every case we can take it for granted that the capacity of one person to direct the emotions of the many is a *charismatic* gift without which trying to initiate political processes is pointless. There is no party without a leader. Lo and behold: the unanimity with which we hold this to be self-evident conceals a troubling assumption – one that we now take for granted and that concerns the very genealogy of democracy. If we accept leader democracies as placidly as we do, it is because we are no longer so troubled by the idea that the emotional origin of political communities is the 'primal horde' and that 'the leader of the mass is still the feared primal father', as Freud warned us.[15] These are all very grave symptoms, as the inhabitants of Vinca so tragically learned in August 1944.

The fact that we unanimously accept the need for the leader as a good thing, and do not understand how *problematic* it is that we lack a detailed, shared reflection on the ways and forms in which leadership materialises, is an excellent example of the new role of political romanticism in the contemporary era.

This is possible because we have been well trained. A very similar dynamic has long been at work in the economic model of neoliberalism, with all the consequences that this model has had for our material life. Of course, we now all recognise – sometimes with almost suspicious conformism – that neoliberalism represents a qualitative leap insofar as it has been able to transform our identities, their underlying meanings, our passions. If we tried to list only the titles of some of the major sociological analyses of the contemporary age, we would find an almost superfluous reference to this qualitative leap, which concerns an *emotional* institutionalisation of society. Here are just a few of these titles: *The Uneasy Society, Excited Society, The High-Speed Society, Burnout Society.*[16] This notwithstanding, when it comes to elaborating proposals alternative to the current government of the economy,[17] we tend to consider credible those proposals that deal exclusively with 'material production processes' and 'empirical data' such as tiny fluctuations in growth, the ups and downs of the stock market, and so on, to the point of reducing the crisis of capitalism to the only seemingly 'rational' object there is: currency (and its sovereignty). In short, when we recognise the depth of the transformations that neoliberalism has carried out, we accept without protest the argument that this is much more than a shift of sovereignty from political to economic government – rather, it involves an overall government of our *forms of life.* And yet, when it comes to imagining alternative, critical processes, we are unable to provide ourselves with any tools for responding to neoliberal romanticism other than the instruments of political realism.

There is therefore a problem that concerns our emotional sphere and affects both the political and the economic dimension. The more these dimensions use emotions, the less we feel the need to take care of them. A little as Schmitt was doing in relation to political romanticism, when it comes to public life we, too, still tend 'to regard romanticism itself as [no]thing other than a "reactionary" element in modern life, a phenomenon with its roots in the past and doomed to extinction at the hands of the rational elements in culture and society'.[18] Perhaps it is worth recognising that this temptation – which still orients a good part of the judgements and political projects we are capable of – no longer withstands either the test of history or the test of our individual lives, as consumer capitalism has shown with reasonable clarity.

With today's insight, the most important value of reflection on the age of consumption is that it has understood – probably belatedly – that the rationalist optimism of the classical economists did not sufficiently take into consideration capitalism's affective grip on our individual lives. If modern consumption has indeed accomplished a transformation, it consists in having represented an irresistible mechanism of individual self-definition that uses the power of individual passions and the material and symbolic seduction of commodities. Which is to say: it consists in having revealed that *homo oeconomicus* is far from being exclusively or primarily anti-romantic, but rather defines herself first and foremost (but not only) through her romanticism.

Our passions have been mobilised as the fodder for lighting up the 'rationality' of capitalism and for allowing it to govern our everyday strategies, our behaviours, and their motivations.[19] This mobilisation has been prepared through consumption, which ranges from the great marketplaces and supermarkets to private spaces and screens, from the single model of the 1960s – *one* television, *one* telephone, *one* car – to the multiplication, necessary to capitalism's survival and growth, of the same object of consumption.

It would be mistaken to believe that this process is a matter of everything being flattened down to the single dimension of economic life. The predominant vision of economic life today expands through the individualised supply of passions, of rights and, above all, of freedoms. Our experience of freedom thus becomes paradoxical. On the one hand, it re-elaborates the founding concept of the liberal tradition: negative freedom, that is, freedom from external limits and interference of any kind. On the other hand, it gets excited by the possibility of having everything that seems to be available to us but has in fact been already decided upon by others. To experience freedom today would consist of the power of no longer choosing anything. As one advert recently put out on Italian TV emphasises, 'new technologies are giving us the freedom not to have to choose'.

The neoliberal age has made the principal intuition of consumerism – creating profit from the exploitation of the sphere of passions – a precision job. We need only think of the contemporary spread of video games (in fact they are no longer called that!), where the romanticism of passions is exhibited in the possibility of identifying with genuinely romantic heroes: medieval knights, contemporary warriors, and so on.

If this is indeed the case, it may be useful to think of the historical phase we are living in terms of a *neoliberal romanticism*, that is, a period in which this romantic seduction, which began with consumption and was used as a mechanism of individual self-definition, has become distinctive and almost *natural*. Homo oeconomicus *has become an incorrigible romantic.*

Certainly neoliberalism is not simply a variation on the theme of consumer capitalism. To understand fully what we are getting at, it is useful to identify the interpretative thread that links the romanticism of consumption to the romanticism of the neoliberal individual.

In a fine book dedicated to the modern consumerist

spirit, Colin Campbell emphasises in a distinct manner the idea that consumer society is not just that specific social scene where each person can acquire objects to satisfy her own inexhaustible desires. This is not simply a matter of having everything we desire within our grasp, but a matter of being able always to desire *afresh*. Thus the novelty of modern consumption is the constant production of 'new' desires through the continual cycle of goods. Two characteristic traits work side by side here: the *massification* of goods; and, at the same time, the *individualisation* of the desires that drive consumption. Although these are seemingly opposite tendencies, massification and individualisation are reconciled in the romantic idea that I can access commodities and products that are designed exclusively for me and that grant me the slight, breezy joy of being simultaneously *unique* and *equal*.

For this reason consumer capitalism has been an era of transition. Indeed, during these years, capitalism's capacity to forge a model of society has rapidly specialised in more than organising the cycle of production and the sale of objects, namely in a genuine social institutionalisation of the forms of individual life.

The romantic ethics of consumer capitalism has not made the world of things into a projection of an already predefined narcissism, but rather – through increase in the number of things to be desired – has produced ever new forms of satisfying the self. This is anything but an antimodern or regressive romanticism! The constant presentation of new commodities allows our identities to shift, to change, to progress. The real object that consumerism produces is not simply goods, but our own egos: no longer does the individual invent reality in a haphazard way, as Schmitt feared. Rather it is reality, in its overabundant and variegated supply, that allows the individual constantly to renovate herself (or to lose her way). It *permits* or it *compels* – and these are no longer so very different options.

We should begin by saying that neoliberal romanticism has removed the mask of this consumerist mechanism; it has, however, also left us with the illusion of being sovereign consumers so as to compel us, when our choices concern essential events, to see ourselves as passive end users in the service of phantoms that regenerate and impose themselves relentlessly, of always precarious images of our own egos – which are to be reinvented, redefined and imposed. The ego is a phantom that we obsess about compulsively. And the effort to imagine this phantom not only disconnects us from the world but seems to be the only means still left to us of constructing the world socially. That is the ego's only possibility of 'living in society' (and also of 'engaging in politics'). Here is the new history of education – *Bildungsgeschichte*. It is a construct of the individual consciousness that is always on the brink of collapse and is not anchored to any public space of mediation, conflict and shared decision.

Invoking Habermas, Michel Foucault briefly described like this the ways in which technique conditions reality:

One can distinguish three major types of techniques in human societies: the techniques which permit one to produce, to transform, to manipulate things; the techniques which permit one to use sign systems; and the techniques which permit one to determine the conduct of individuals, to impose certain wills on them, and to submit them to certain ends or objectives.[20]

While this is a rather summary division, it is nonetheless a useful one. In the transition that has taken us from consumerism to neoliberal romanticism, the structure of production has itself been redefined, shifting its centre from the production of objects and signs (the first two types of techniques, that defined consumer society and the society of the spectacle)[21] to those techniques that determine individuals' conduct through a teleological discipline – in other words, through a genuine science of the passions (desires and impulses) that is able to define and to shape the objectives on the basis of which we make choices and orient our behaviours.

Mobilising passions

Neoliberal romanticism has made use of political romanticism's ambiguity – the same one that raised Schmitt's suspicions. It has done so by *partly taming it* and *by putting its main centres to work for itself.*

The transformation of the political value of individual freedom shows how this partial domestication has taken place. For the romantic hero, this liberty took on a political character insofar as it had a deep transgressive meaning: the political value of freedom lay in the capacity to challenge a rigidly established social order. As we noted a few pages back, most such examples gave rise to a genuine 'civic project'. We could say that, in political romanticism, individual feeling was the most powerful instrument for putting the universal norm in question. Neoliberal romanticism has depoliticised the demands for individual freedom: the sentiment that directs them is not a desire for transformation but an urge to acquire. Having been depoliticised, the romantic passions are now domesticated: as Foucault suggests, neoliberalism functions by relentlessly producing and consuming freedom.[22]

In this whirlwind of domestication, the things that stir our passions are still similar to the great mythologies of historical romanticism: the journey, the dream, the incessant search for change, the idealisation of extreme feelings. Looking at this with today's eyes, we have to say that there is no era more romantic than neoliberalism, which has made these great mythologies of desire ever more popular and accessible. What is completely different is the process of appropriating them and the value that we draw from them. The possibility of acquiring them is always within reach, and this makes us competitive and performative. Their value is not that they allow a transformation of our identity, but rather that they offer a validation that has to be constantly claimed and obtained. We are guided by the exclusive passion for recognition, not by the passion of self-discovery.

We might believe that neoliberal romanticism no longer has any connection with the political sphere, precisely because of its depoliticisation – unless, that is, politics itself has been contaminated by this domestication and dominated by depoliticised passions.[23] We have in mind the way in which, in the construction of a large proportion of political projects, the urge to acquire takes the lead over the desire for transformation. The objective here is no longer to transform the present state of things, but to make a bid to appropriate power for oneself and for one's political 'side', even if the price of this appropriation is in fact the impossibility of transforming things.

Political Romanticism and Neoliberal Romanticism

Political realism's quite legitimate argument that the appropriation of power is the necessary condition for transforming society is inverted in a paradoxical romanticism of power: the desire for it ends up negating any political rationality.[24] Politics, too, ends up as the stage for the repetitive compulsion to conquer a power that has lost any transformative value, whose only function – entirely economic – is to allow politicians to defeat the competition and to see themselves reflected in the power they alone possess. Politics is, then, no exception: it, too, is almost exclusively dominated by the model of the entrepreneur of the self. 'Not a supermarket society, but an enterprise society', observes Foucault.[25] It is no coincidence that a ruthless principle of political competition (we call it transfer of power) has imposed itself exactly when the variety of political 'products', with their different contents and persons, has been so reduced. The logic of the enterprise defines not only the oligarchical manner in which parties are organised, but also the emotional investment of individual politicians. The politician works away at building up her political credit as if it were capital from which she could make profits for herself alone. A party doesn't look like a social enterprise any more; it looks merely like a personal one.

The same domestication is at work in the contemporary use of human sympathy. As scholars have noted, Adam Smith made the latter into a foundational principle of modern anthropology. For the Scottish philosopher its role was very clear. Sympathy was delegated the difficult task of setting down social limits within which the economic exercise of natural selfishness could be deployed in virtuous fashion.

Mobilising passions

How selfish soever man may be supposed, there are evidently some principles in his nature, which interest him in the fortune of others, and render their happiness necessary to him, though he derives nothing from it except the pleasure of seeing it.[26]

We could hardly say that neoliberal romanticism has not further emphasised the socially orienting role of sympathy. If we asked our little group of teenagers in Vinca (but also those who are not digital natives) in what kind of space the principle of sympathy should be king, they would tell us about the emotional connections they have incessantly looked for and experienced on social networks: a gigantic experiment in *individual narrations* that are based on the principle of human sympathy. Besides, we are not so far here from what Smith suggested: social networks are romantic mechanisms in which we *participate* in others' lives through the pleasure of *contemplation*. Where, then, is the danger in domesticating passions and setting them to work? As the libertarian utopias at the base of the earliest hacker ethics well remind us, this sympathy operates in an (apparently) de-institutionalised space. It needs no mediation. The seductive power of social networks also results from the fact that there is no mediation between me and the other: the relation between us is left to our own devices. Paradoxically, this libertarian utopia has served to renew the value of the social role of sympathy, to connect it with the principle of individual freedom, or even to experiment with new forms of gift-based exchange.[27]

And yet sympathy, in its version as a positive passion, has many deficiencies; this politically free use of the web is reserved to a few elites. For the rest, the common experience of social networks points in a quite different direction: no publicly debated norm and no discussion of our common life. If you think about it, the proprietary sentiment that governs the upkeep of our Facebook "walls" is something rather curious. On the one hand, we stir up a quantitative, performative impulse by widening the audience of observers, by seeking to extend our contacts, by increasing the number of potential followers who will see the items we publish as if they were traces of our own selves. We want to receive recognition from the many. But on the other hand we defend our wall from being disturbed by those who do not think the same way as we do; and for this we use a strange proprietary argument evocative of serious political battles and which, also for this reason, seems at least a little suspicious: 'the wall is mine and I will keep it as I like'.

By emphasising that our individual freedom is a genuine relation of ownership, we risk sinking into what some analysts have defined as a 'deep romantic chasm'.[28] In this 'chasm' there is a real construction of social reality, which must not in any way take institutional form. The depoliticisation of human sympathy is thus a condition of access to social networks. Politics does appear in this context, but at most as an object of exchange that defines relations and sympathies. Take the politicians' emphasis on the need to use social media platforms. Does this not, for the most part end up becoming a simple tactic of their communications strategy? Democracy 2.0 often limits itself to making politics an object of contemplation, not an art that defines the modes of participation.

In another sense, this marginalisation of politics is only a superficial development. In reality, that public space is codified by private laws. Whoever joins a social network agrees to norms whose deliberation is not an object of sympathy or of public discussion. This is how sympathy becomes an irresistible passional motor that speeds up the circulation of digital capitalism. It loses political meaning and acquires an ever greater economic significance. It produces information useful for the valorisation of capital. It puts us to work even when we are not at work.

When digital capitalism sets us to work, one of the consequences is to change the very direction of time, by comparison to that of political romanticism. We can explain this change by turning to a contemporary novel that portrays a wholly classical romanticism, Orhan Pamuk's *The Museum of Innocence*. As many readers will know, this novel tells a love story (and the story of a happy life) by listing a series of traces of memory, of things. But the secret of this long inventory is that it is made up of moments; it is not made of a permanence, as Aristotle thought.[29] The late eighteenth-century romantics would have described it as a series of 'spots of time'.[30] The intensity of these moments is, inevitably, followed by the 'time of retreat'. Memory and regret filled the romantics' days, their months, even their years. This was the romantics' *long* time, the price to pay for the exceptional character of the 'spots of time' – a time that seemed infinite and was difficult to bear under *le soleil noir de la mélancholie* ['the black sun of melancholy'].[31]

All this emphasised the emotional role of the interval, of the empty space, of the time that went to *waste*. Classic romanticism demanded a time in which one could be consumed by the absence of the happy moment, so that one could then enjoy its exceptional occurrence.

Conversely, neoliberal romanticism postulates an *accelerated* conception of time, which revisits the romantic myth of speed. This is a permanent connection, which allows no economic waste, no empty spaces, no loose ends. Following an inexorable rhythm, every moment must be conducive to the acquisition of recognition. Unable to keep this pace even though we are permanently connected, we feel a sort of 'time famine':

> Perhaps the most surprising and unexpected aspect of social acceleration is the contagious 'time famine' of modern (western) societies. In modernity, social actors have the constant impression that their time is escaping them, that it is too short. It seems that time is perceived as a raw material to be consumed, such as petrol, and, just like it, it is becoming ever rarer and more expensive.[32]

This connection between the need to be permanently connected and the perception of a 'time famine' is worth bearing in mind. Let us offer just two examples.

The first is exquisitely political (and we will return to it in the next chapter). Political discussions have crossed over onto the Internet, and they often unfold at the pace set by mailing lists. Anyone who has had the misfortune of chancing upon one of these mailing lists is well aware of how alienating it is to experience the rate they go at. On the one hand, there is an exponential proliferation of correspondence – the result of being permanently connected (which, of course, applies only to a privileged few). This gives the illusion of being able to exert individual control over every particular word or question and, by so doing, of rendering the delegate function of democracy an anachronism. Each person can finally represent herself *in each and every moment*. On the other

hand, we can only feel a sense of impotence, for the multiplication of actors, of writing, of themes of discussion,
and of personal conflicts (which now become the object
of public email lists) ends up making the time available
absolutely insufficient. Continual connection becomes
an ideal means of busying ourselves with all those things
that lack any real political importance, which increases
our frustration. We might say that, as far as political communications are concerned, the acceleration of
technology – which has transferred spoken and written
correspondence to the proximity of our inboxes, ever
within reach – has had the perverse effect of producing
a sense of time famine. *This acceleration should have
represented the opportunity for an abundance of participation; but in the end it demonstrated that participation
has reached an impasse.*

The second example illuminates perfectly the social
and psychological consequences of this mounting time
famine in the age of its acceleration. As many analysts
have emphasised, after we have been put to work like
this – in a labour that demands that we are constantly
connected – when we go offline, we are no longer able to
sleep.[33] There is a constant rise in sleep disorders. And
sleep represents the pinnacle of 'empty space', that vital
time that cannot be colonised and dominated from the
outside, and that preserves a romantic activity par excellence: dreaming.

Picking up on the themes of romanticism, whatever
their ambiguities, is useful in that it allows us not only
to reflect on a different connection between passional
and political life but also to recognise that, without this
reflection, we cannot fully understand the metamorpho-
sis that has been underway for years.

What, for Schmitt, represented the superiority of realism in the face of political romanticism, today represents its impotence in the face of neoliberal romanticism: that is, the conviction that politics has to treat passions with disdain rather than seek a proper way of governing them and taking care of them. While neoliberalism, as it comes increasingly close to the model of 'positive liberalism' indicated by Foucault,[34] works to use the passions to shield its own hegemony, those who make the step toward politics are no longer concerning themselves with their own passions.

Instead of this, we should be imagining innovative models for the political government of passions and of our own selves – a government capable of constructing a true and proper space of political critique.

3

Politics and Passions, Today

Constitutional wisdom

In an article published a few years ago, Mukulika Banerjee focuses on the impassioned mass participation in elections in India (around 700 million voters and 8 million polling stations). India is not just anywhere. In this enormous country inequalities are engraved by the indelible marks of the caste system; and democracy does not seem to be in rude health. Nonetheless, Banerjee's article describes a mounting enthusiasm for electoral processes, in megalopolises as in the ever-extending suburbs. But what is particularly interesting for our purposes is the thesis that the author advances as an explanation of this phenomenon:

> The vote is felt to possess both symbolic power, in expressing people's self-respect and self-worth, and instrumental power, in helping to ward off potential attacks by the state upon that self-worth. The vital importance of such power for dignity and survival, along with the appealing formal

equality of the vote's operation and the sense of dutiful participation as citizen-subjects which it affords, together generate that deep-felt sense of 'something sacred' which gives a moral and emotional core to the ritual elements of the election and draws India's voters irresistibly towards it.[1]

In short, passions are the essential impulse that drives Indians to activity at election time. Participating in elections improves self-esteem and self-respect and allows Indian citizens to defend themselves from state attacks. This feeling of satisfaction and *increased power* is what gives back to democracy – at its defining point – the sacred tone that we used to know so well in Europe a little while ago. In some places and at some specific times, democracy is still able to capture people's passions and proves its power to increase the dignity of each person. This brief journey via India prompts certain conclusions, which will serve as foreword to chapter 3.

The first conclusion is that, when we refer to categories such as anti-politics, post-democracy and the crisis of politics, we often risk passing judgement on the present without a historical perspective. And history is the master of the concept, in that it tends to relativize our absolute points of view and put them in the necessary perspective. There is still a strong element of Eurocentrism in the idea that the wearing out of *democracy* – and we started out by taking this as a self-evident fact – is the universal meaning that we ought to assign to the historical and plural experience of *democracies*.

The second conclusion is that *decentring* our gaze (that is, not presuming that our own perspective on the state of democracy is the only possible one) is also a way to restore hope. Sometimes when we look at contemporary politics we are possessed by a destructive spirit: its decline is taken not as the signal of a contest that is still being fought out, but as the indicator of a failure that has already happened and is irreversible. This is to fail to recognise that we, too – the wayward inhabitants of the so-called post-democracies – do not yet know what really comes *after* this democracy of ours, even though it is imperfect, downgraded, fundamentally based on inequality and, especially in its most recent versions, profoundly disappointing.[2]

The final conclusion is, in some regards, the one that can least be taken for granted. For in the Indian case and in Banerjee's description of it there is a certain indication that is not without analogy with what we are working toward. Democracy has a power of attraction not only when it is working, but above all when it gives everyone the feeling that they can contribute to its functioning. That is, when it is still able to provide a narrative that justifies the choice to engage politically as an enrichment of our everyday life and not as its constant frustration. If our crisis of politics is also a crisis of passions, then the confidence that we mentioned in the Indian case is a *strange political form of passion*.

Even in Italy we need to recover what was once defined as the democratic ideal. For many decades it fed on two brilliant regulating ideas: legitimation and equality. These are the same two ideas that fire enthusiasm in India: the idea of being able to exercise real control over the state, and the feeling that in politics we can still seek to extend the conditions of equality, especially by actively participating in political decisions.

In Europe, both these ideas seem to be irreversibly in crisis. Small groups no longer take too much care to legitimise themselves. The vote seems to be a still usable space of participation, but its capacity to alter the terms of government is less and less decisive. Other paths now legitimate increasingly narrow groups to govern increasingly large ones.

The counter-reforming tendencies today underway in the European democracies seem above all concerned to fix procedures that will allow for the formal competition – elections – to *stop* being a tool by which we periodically put power back in dispute. And, even if the parties passionately declare their differences with one another, they are not at all so different. This represses that feeling of heightened power that we get at the moment of going to the polling station. There thus develops an increasing overlap between power and narrow oligarchies. The place of power is always *occupied*, and the legitimising function of the vote is now an *empty* one. When, repeatedly and ostentatiously, these narrow oligarchies show that they and power are the same thing, there is more than a whiff of passional vice at hand.

As for equality – the second 'brilliant regulating idea', after legitimation – there now remains very little of the myth of a level playing field equal for all electoral competitors, such as would guarantee them the same resources and the same possibilities of reaching power. We seem to have left behind the idea that the subjects par excellence of politics – parties – have the essential task of encouraging the equal distribution of power by serving the principle of participation by the greatest number, as Article 49 of the Italian Constitution specifies:

Machiavellian monkeys

All citizens have the right to freely associate in parties to contribute to determining national policies through democratic processes. (http://www.quirinale.it/allegati_statici/costituzione/costituzione_inglese.pdf)

This is a profound piece of wisdom; the parties' role is not exclusively limited to some people's exercising power on behalf of others but is also measured by their capacity to guarantee and find effective forms that will allow the greater number of citizens to associate freely. But, even if we did want to return to this constitutional wisdom, what would we need to do?

Machiavellian monkeys

Let's imagine that one of those girls we met in Vinca, in the Apuan mountains so beloved of the nineteenth-century romantics, decided to try finding out what happens at traditional political meetings. Thus far her hesitant desire for political participation has been satiated by information found on the web, by opinion pieces, comments and discussions on social networks – above all, by a series of sensitive topics and priorities chosen according to a logic to which we are not accustomed. A difficult-to-understand logic, with a reordering effect: a logic that keeps together political questions that we traditionally thought to be in conflict with one another, mixing social and civil rights, redistribution and recognition, and no longer making distinctions between the material and the immaterial sphere.

Politics, structured as it is through its languages, its practices and its relations (and therefore also its decisions), seems not to have taken heed yet of all this. It prefers to proceed by way of rituals that are sacrosanct but a bit worn down and redundant: assemblies, appeals that resort to a state of emergency by now permanent (as if we did not properly understand, in childhood, the fable of the boy who cried 'wolf!'). In reality, all these rituals of 'participation' stand at the margins of the politics that really decides: the politics of leaders, of TV programmes, of castes and unelected powers that now shamelessly distort democratic decision-making. So, unlike the impassioned voters in India, the girl from Vinca shares the same impotence that we do. All the remaining forms of political participation, old or new, seem to have been disconnected from decision-making power. Political oligarchies instrumentalise 'participation' with an emphasis equivalent to the insignificance to which it has been for the most part reduced.

So, if we did have to go to a political meeting, we would face one first difficulty: we no longer know where and when to associate politically. Political 'meetings' have been replaced by political 'events'. It is not difficult to recognise, in this spectacularisation of politics, a limitation of the power of participation, which is reduced to an element of political marketing and left unable to shape processes and decisions. Whoever does participate is a spectator or a passive consumer. Nothing corresponds today to the substance of the task assigned by the constitution: a free association, with democratic methods, with a view to shaping national politics. The very definition of a 'light party'* seems to explain this difficulty. It is a party that increases its number

---

* A party without 'heavy' internal structures, a term coined to refer to Silvio Berlusconi's Forza Italia.

of votes (not that this helps it to respect voter choices afterwards, of course) while it reduces its number of activists. It is practically an anti-constitutional party, insofar as the constitution assigns parties the task of associating citizens.

But suppose that we managed, miraculously, to pick out a meeting place – perhaps a *sezione* [a local branch of a political party, or a social club office, or both together], if they still exist – where a gathering has been organised. At the end of a day of study or work, our young friend arrives on time at the meeting. She finds no one there – a bad omen. She will have to wait for a good while before the meeting starts. Perhaps this will not be just dead time. It will be an opportunity to chat and exchange messages without too many distractions.

This late start seems a ritual from some ancient ceremonial, when politics was a strong passion and the rhythm of life was clearly marked by a social beat: work and, in the evening, political engagement (for men). Today this doesn't hold any more. When there is work – and in fact even when there isn't – it follows us home, waiting for us on our computer screen after dinner. Even in privileged places such as the university, working time seems to have become continuous: emails are a constant torrent and no one has any qualms about phoning to ask a question even if the hour is late or the weekend has already arrived. Work is increasingly intermittent, without guarantees, unrecognised and unpaid.

Despite this, we are full-time workers. Even the most fortunate are forced to finish a project, without any timetable to help them to impose existential boundaries. The permanently connected computer is an office without hours, while an increasing bureaucratisation multiplies the operations we have to perform in order to finish anything. Both offer themselves up for exploitation by setting us to work for free in our free time. As for the others, they are workers in a weary and constant search for work. What seems to come after the end of labour society – where work played the essential function of public identification – is a society of workers without work. Arendt already prophesied it, albeit with different arguments.[3]

It is worth recognising clearly that the true critique of the party form is not of a moral (the parties are colonised by worn-out oligarchies), aesthetic (the parties are not the most fit containers for attracting participation) or realist order (the parties are no longer able to manage power), but of a social one: the party form is still conceived of in such a way as to represent labour society, and has no idea what sort of thing a society of workers without work might be. We could quite legitimately imagine that the crisis of parties is, far more than a crisis of the credibility of the individuals who represent them today, a dissonance of the forms, of the languages, of the relations, and ultimately of the passions that political aggregations repeat without examining their conscience or their history.

This conceptual difference hardens into a very concrete separation: the first thing that the girl from Vinca will notice is that she finds herself in a place where there are no young people—a place occupied instead by political professionals and pensioners. The former fulfil their dream of busying themselves with politics full time (the worse democracy gets, the more aspiring politicians present themselves to the electorate); the latter are aided by their lack of other commitments and are full of rancor and sadness as they review the central decades of their lives, when they were active but dependent on power – a dependence they did not want, or were unable, to defend themselves from.[4] All of them are unable to recognise that the entrenched rituals of political life to which they are so accustomed are now unsustainable for those who have seen the rhythms of their everyday lives turned upside down by the neoliberal reorganisation. The disorientated gaze of those who wait for the discussion to begin even as they are assailed by the tiredness of the day is the first indicator of a not-only-political crisis of politics; of its incapacity to realign itself with the life cycle of the unprivileged; of a politics that refuses even to ask itself the question in these terms. What are the forms, the languages and the passions that can allow a worker without work to associate freely and to engage in politics? This is no simple exercise in style, but (in our view) one of those questions that are fundamental to resetting credible political processes, at long last.

The political discussion finally begins. The interventions seem to be directed by an established script that follows unwritten customs. Not all interventions are equal, to start with. In political meetings, equality is not a category of politics. If all were equal, no doubt some would be *more equal* than others.

Then there is an agenda and rules that speakers must follow (for instance, an equal amount of time allotted to each person). It is quite noticeable, if rather a surprise, that those who slate others for not 'respecting the rules' are the ones who never stop talking. It is as if in politics the ego were now a permanent state of exception (as we shall soon explain). Then, when someone has intervened, he does not sit down to listen to the others. He usually stays on his feet at the back of the room and goes on chatting with his comrades, taking no interest in what is being said by anyone not known or not affiliated through political history or group belonging. Seeing the composition of the participants, even as she attends for the first time, the young woman from Vinca will sense that there is a complicated tangle of private and public histories: that these assemblies are mainly hangouts for old friends – and also for old enemies – who have been meeting for decades, passing from one failed project to the next. In every sphere, and politics is certainly no exception, those who dominate are elites who often sacrifice the instinct for procreation, heredity and legacy to their own narcissism. They select the leadership of the future through the single criterion of repetition, not of critical differentiation. Anything but a world without fathers! It seems to be a world made up *only* of fathers and sons, without grown-ups (women are present but most often in subservient positions), where what prevails is either an uncritical attachment to some or the rituality of suspicion, envy or mistrust. No one can feel welcome in such a context – least of all someone who is struggling to find her political identity and does not need to defend it at all costs.

In a few compelling pages of introduction to his volume on evolutionism, Telmo Pievani imagines an 'alien scientist' who lands in a political meeting and, aghast at this spectacle, asks an 'evolutionary psychologist' for some explanation.[5] Our girl from Vinca would probably react not much differently from the alien. Both of them come from another world and are pitched into contexts in which the forms and languages of representation are organised according to the patterns and orders of a world that is no more.

The danger we risk falling into, if we do not begin once more to call into question the prevalent governance of passions in politics, is the latter's *naturalisation*.[6] Pievani uses a striking expression when he introduces the image of 'Machiavellian monkeys' in this regard. There is something worrying – as well as comical – in the observation that today the arenas of politics have become so wild that we can draw an analogy between the behaviours of our *representatives* and the instincts of monkeys.

This all has an explanation of sorts, which allows us at least to keep our worries under control. The nature of the political human – the object of Machiavelli's reflection – has now become human nature *tout court*. The politician is the completely passional human, ignorant of any responsibility in the area of self-government and mastery over the passions. And this is just like the neoliberal. It is this naturalisation that makes us into monkeys adapted to politics. But is politics still up to the task of building spaces and languages able to emancipate us from the passions of the present? Does not perhaps the reversal of Von Clausewitz's thesis – politics is the continuation of war by other means, and no longer the other way around[7] – make room for a model of governance of the passions that contaminates politics with the most pervasive forms and modalities of neoliberalism? In the last resort, what would it take for the girl from Vinca to become passionate about politics without necessarily transforming herself into a Machiavellian monkey?

In the pages of Pievani's book, this is how the 'alien scientist' refutes the exclusively naturalist interpretations of the 'evolutionary psychologist':

No one has ever seen chimpanzees founding a party and getting into a fight as soon as it has got started, tearing lumps out of each other so as to minimise everyone's chances of winning the elections and thus reaching the summit of the hierarchy of dominance. In fact this is a disadaptive behaviour that consists of systematically inflicting harm on the other members of your group without drawing any benefit from doing so, and even making it easier for the rival group to succeed.[8]

In short, we cannot give credit to an explanation according to which human beings, once thrown into a political context, necessarily reveal their nature as Machiavellian monkeys, both because the monkeys would not behave like this – monkeys' instinct is directed towards adaptive strategies, which necessarily include collaborative, non-destructive ones – and because Machiavelli was well aware that political practices demand rather more complex passional styles. As one of the most famous passages in *The Prince* puts it:

> Many have pictured republics and principalities which in fact have never been known or seen, because how one lives is so far distant from how one ought to live, that he who neglects what is done for what ought to be done, sooner effects his ruin than his preservation; for a man who wishes to act entirely up to his professions of virtue soon meets with what destroys him among so much that is evil.
>
> Hence it is necessary for a prince wishing to hold his own to know how to do wrong, and to make use of it or not according to necessity.[9]

The lesson of the Florentine *consigliere* seems to suggest a complex and refined exercise of self-government on the part of the politician, to be practised in the sphere of her affective life. Machiavelli was in fact suggesting to the prince not that he should never make a 'profession of good' but that he should be careful not to do it always ('in all regards'). There is, then, a good and a bad use of passions, depending on whether they serve the good or they demonstrate hostility or cynicism. In either case, these passions have to be put into context. The politician is not the person who is good or bad, but the person who governs passions correctly, on the basis of the conditions he encounters, as necessity requires. This is what Machiavelli suggests: the good politician is not the most violent, the most cynical, the most powerful or the most shameless. Rather he is the most cunning: he is the one able to understand which means are the most appropriate for enrolling the passions in the service of circumstances and their demands. Machiavelli's whole argument culminates in this final suggestion: 'Hence it is necessary for a prince wishing to hold his own to know how to do wrong, and to make use of it or not according to necessity.'

Developing an emotional wisdom is a quality essential to the proper exercise of politics. Clearly, for Machiavelli the politician should practice governing the passions in the context of generalised warfare. But in this model of permanent conflict there is also a need for states of peace, of winning trust for oneself, of tying alliances, of training one's own passions in the right measure given what is at stake. We could summarise this in one line: political realism neither replaces nor resoves the government of passions, but rather demands it and imposes it as its own condition.

A few centuries later, Machiavellianism – and not

Machiavelli himself[10] – reduced this refined exercise of politics to the pure domination of the tyrant (we need only remember the definition of Machiavellianism as presented in Diderot's *Encyclopédie*: 'A detestable kind of politics that can be defined in short as the art of being a tyrant').[11] When we speak of political realism today – often justifying its necessity in the name of the latest emergency – we mainly do so in precisely this sense, hence failing to pay attention to emotional life. We are convinced that political realism is a matter of exercising an external dominion, of 'taking power' – no more, no less – and we do not take care of the relational practices through which power is attained, of the languages and codes that are privileged, or of the gigantic removal of the physical sphere that makes the seizure of power a further residue of the male domination over the female.

The reduction of the affective life of politics to that of Machiavellian monkeys ends up making us complicit in the neoliberal system of domination. To put it simply: we still nurture the illusion that we can change the forms of power, even as our forms of life have, quietly, been taken hostage. It may therefore be useful to embark upon a closer study of the readjustment of politics as democracy's regulating ideas are reduced to the neoliberal order – which is also happening on the terrain of passions. Politics not only loses its critical – transformative function but sets itself up as an obstinate protector of that order and of its mode of governing the passions. It does so by rejecting the regulating ideas that have strengthened the various experiences of democracy in recent centuries – first and foremost, legitimation and equality. This is true of both representative and participatory democracy. The permanent crisis of politics is also the crisis of the passions mobilised in these forms of democracy.

The dignity of the politician

In the last decades of the nineteenth century, when a struggle for the vote was underway all over Europe, representative democracy was considered an objective to be achieved. In the course of those battles, an exalted and exaggerated power came to be ascribed to parliamentary assemblies. In his 1861 *Considerations on Representative Government*, John Stuart Mill wrote that parliament had 'to be at once the nation's Committee of Grievances and its Congress of Opinions; an arena ... [w]here every person in the country may count upon finding somebody who speaks his mind as well or better than he could speak it himself'.[12]

This fervent wish had little to do with reality, both in Mill's day and later on. Parliaments have given progressively greater proof of their dark sides: their vulnerability to pressure from lobbying, their manipulation and corruption, their heavy bureaucracy and regulations, and their subordination to party-political priorities and individuals' careers. As we have just seen, outside the parliaments that level playing field of the liberal imaginary, in which everyone aspiring to power enjoys equal opportunities and equal resources, does not exist. Politicians with a dirty conscience continually hark back to this image.

We could even say that Mill's fervid optimism sounds decidedly out of place to the ears of citizens in western democracies. It represents an idealisation of representation, and one that clashes with the evidence provided by behaviours.

A few decades later, Max Weber showed himself well aware of the risky consequences that politicians' malign use of the passions could have on the credibility of a representative government. In a short 1919 talk dedicated to politics as profession he tried to respond to some questions that are decidedly of interest to our own book. What are the passions peculiar to a politician? And what dangers do these passions prefigure? He was perfectly aware that politics is a science that cannot be governed simply through good intentions or the right passions. It is not enough to sanitise the list of politically useful passions. For Weber, in fact, politics has a diabolical characteristic that transcends any particular era:

> Also the early Christians knew full well that the world is governed by demons and that he who lets himself in for politics, that is, for power and force as means, contracts with diabolical powers and for his action it is not true that good can follow only from good and evil only from evil, but that often the opposite is true. Anyone who fails to see this is, indeed, a political infant.[13]

Weber was not at all, then, a critic of political realism – the almost 'mystical' tones of these lines have a strong whiff of political theology – and still less a critic of the idea that there should be, by necessity, small elites that engage in politics just professionally. Nothing could be more distant from an opponent of the traditional forms of representative democracy. And yet we are convinced that he would have had no small amount of mistrust for those politicians who show themselves to be little 'Machiavellian monkeys'. Weber's pages serve as a clear descripion of the pathological drift of the passions mobilised in contemporary political spaces.

First of all, Weber points to the need to take particular care of one's inner state before engaging in politics:

> He who is inwardly defenseless and unable to find the proper answer for himself had better stay away from this career. For in any case, besides grave temptations, it is an avenue that may constantly lead to disappointments.[14]

These words seemingly give credence to the idea that we each need an appropriate government of our inner passions before we can participate in meetings with others. The internal weakness to which Weber refers is very serious, yet little considered. This weakness can be a 'pathological' passion for self-recognition, the result of dissatisfaction, an incapacity for internal dialogue, dependence on other people's judgement, or 'attachment dynamics' gone wrong. In everyday discussions, we tend to evaluate these attitudes under the label 'narcissism'. But narcissism is something a little more complex and is difficult to explain in a few lines. We prefer to concentrate on one of its more specific manifestations, which is quite widespread politically: the pathology of an *unrelenting demand for self-recognition*.[15] What are its consequences? In the first place, because we cannot find the right answers all by ourselves, we end up making the public sphere a shop window in which we constantly put ourselves on display. This takes place not only in the limited sphere of 'official politics', but also in the activity of voluntary associations, NGOs and organised civil society groups. How many times have their meetings been dominated (and ruined) by this type of behaviour, with one person – often a charismatic leader for life

– who never stops talking, even in front of the bored desperation of the other participants?

It is entirely unobjectionable that there is a legitimate demand for recognition in political life, too. A person who achieves proper recognition through his political engagement is certainly a more well-balanced person. This is a discussion very much in fashion in contemporary political theory. We could say that only the experience of being recognised – also in terms of one's own passional nature – allows each one to participate fully in public life. According to this logic, recognition, even of an emotional nature, is a necessary condition for the experience of good political participation.[16]

But the need for *proper recognition* does not have much to do with the *relentless demand for self-recognition*. While the former generates a feeling of confidence, the latter generates perennial rivalry, impatience and resentment. Recognition stops being the emotional condition that allows for participation and becomes instead its unique driving objective. Politics seems to have become a meeting place for individuals who set their own self-realisation as the ultimate purpose of their engagement, sacrificing any patient construction of shared passions. They identify the common good with their own careers, thus justifying all types of behaviour, including the slavish following of the leader. They are the Machiavellian monkeys, all gathered around in service of their Prince.

It thus becomes clear that, alongside good will, legitimate ambition and simple competence, a certain style of governing one's passions should be one of the conditions that determine the dignity of the politician. If self-realisation or the relentless demand for self-recognition are insufficient passions, what are the passions and qualities through which the politician 'can hope to do justice to this power (however narrowly circumscribed it may be in the individual case)? How can he hope to do justice to the responsibility that power imposes upon him?'[17]

Even to take an interest in this subject – the specific dignity of a politician who has been granted a morsel of power – seems out of date. In this respect, contemporary politics has truly given a bad example. At best it has replaced *dignity* with *reputation*. More often it has legitimised the idea that there is no need for people to be worthy of power, that power legitimises itself – which is *exactly* what should not happen in a democracy. The logic of domination is therefore extended, without any concern for responsibility, from the college master who has the teaching staff's fate in his hands to the entrepreneur who can sack workers without any just cause. *The more these power relations are extended and planned out in advance, the less we ask ourselves what might make us worthy of them.* In its contemporary version, class struggle is also inflected in the separation between those who are *paralysed* by power and those who are *excited* by it. This excitement over a *power* that legitimises itself, without anyone asking what makes us *worthy* of it – and, in consequence, always appears as domination – would seem to be one of the passions that neoliberalism uses to the utmost, in order to fix reality in the way it is.

Of course we should, by way of preparation, avoid the danger – typical of any ethics of rigour applied to political science – of a kind of fanaticism about dignity. Obviously the point is not to idealise the figure of the politician but simply to reassert the need for a link between collective responsibility and individual value (and we mean value, not merit). To give an example, one immediate consequence would be to put back at the centre of public debate the urgent question of what should be the criteria for the selection of leaders, beyond mere obedience to the chief.

From our perspective, the first question to address is: Can a politician be worthy of the power she desires, without having taken care of mastering her own passions? So long as the politician does not ask herself the question of how to govern her own passions, she will be forced to suffer an external governance that will shape her conduct, her decisions and, most importantly, her values – negative or positive passions, happy or sad ones. As we already showed in chapter 1, this is not a matter of absolutising particular passions over others but of *combining* them – in such a way as to rehabitu-ate ourselves to a 'political' government of our passions that may credibly stand its ground against the 'despotic' government that neoliberalism has made us come to expect.

Nor do we want to overemphasise the positive effect of having worthy politicians. The politician who *is* worthy – in terms of her relationship with her own passions – will simply be ground down (or thwarted) by the mechanisms of an unworthy system (that is, a system reduced to the unique government of passions). How many times in recent years did bitter disappointment with the broken promises of new leaders and with polit-ical springs that never blossomed surge in the public?

Our proposal intends to indicate not so much the need for a critique of the *politician*'s own passions as the urgent need to rethink how the neoliberal government of passions represses a large part of the space for the critique *of politics*. We are as if suspended within an unhealable fracture between the task of politics and the function of critique.[18] *A critique of politicians serves to distract us from a radical critique of politics*, of what it has become: that is, from a critique of the transformation of its objective processes, of its capacity (or otherwise) for debate, of its relations with economic sovereignty, of its degree of popular representation. It is illusory to imagine that these transformations can be magically spirited away through a politician's mere good intentions.

In this more general perspective, we think it important to emphasise once more that making a distinction between neoliberalism's individualising passions and the common passions specific to democracy is itself a way of reactivating our critical capacity.

Let's focus on this distinction for a moment. Spinoza wrote that pride is 'pleasure springing from a man thinking too highly of himself'.[19] We could first of all observe that here Spinoza points to an illusory use of joyous passions – a use that is typical of neoliberalism. As we have already observed, its political effect is to direct our collective decisions and our relations towards excessive self-recognition. We have to start giving credit again to that extraordinary capacity to proliferate our active power and joy through connections. This is what Spinoza called the great conquest of democracy; and it goes far beyond a politics based on that excessive sense of self that Spinoza called *arrogance* and Weber *vanity*.

Certainly, shared passions are not free of political risks. They still represent the fuel for the flame of nationalism, of closed communities and of *regressive* challenges to the present neoliberal order. One has, then, to imagine them as real democratic passions able to break out of the impotence (or super-potence) of the individual, to transform atomised anger into a common conflict, to be forms of disidentification and not the mere encrustation of smaller identities into similarly hostile, only bigger ones. Above all, one has to cultivate those *specific* common passions that can allow us to revitalise the great values of the democratic ideal, which neoliberal government has obscured.[20]

The double crisis of passions: Representation and participation

Many will object that this proposal of ours is not very realistic politically, given that modern politics is by definition linked to the exercise of a certain degree of domination and hence compelled to raise in a realistic manner the question of taking power. Without doubt, the rethinking we urgently need, so that we can finally break out of the crisis of representative democracy, is not a matter of any traditional government of passions. If our girl from Vinca really wants to engage in politics, she, too, would have to accustom herself to the rationality of power, to its backlighting and to what is to be read between the lines of discourses. Otherwise she will leave the field open to the political professionals or to their young epigones (just as in the university: the few young people admitted to the feast are often nothing but a faithful mirror image of their teachers, an extension of their vanity) – who have already introjected this rationality of power as a genuine habitus.

A renewed focus on the passions that orient our

choices and our political engagement helps to coun-
terbalance the force of the neoliberal project, which
concerns itself not so much with the means as with the
ends. What is politics *useful for*, in this context? What
passion can mobilise political engagement and impose
controls on the legitimate aspiration for power? We
need to change the role of passions in politics, to try
out forms of relating and practices of language that are
really an alternative to neoliberalism and its colonisation of our own internal life; and to place at the centre
of our engagement inclusive passions that have the
capacity to create links, not to break or terrorise them.
All this is a way of putting at the heart of political
engagement, as a matter of urgency, the questioning of
its *purpose*. A politics of potential can no longer give
rise to this questioning all by itself.

It is as if, in politics at the present moment, we were
unable to imagine anything except two ideal types of
politician. On the one hand there is the *rational* politician, who knows how to use the passions rationally and
does not let herself be dominated by them. On the other
hand, there is the politician who displays a certain type
of passions typical of neoliberalism: she is competitive
and has no interest in building connections unless they
take the form of domination, dependency, voluntary
servitude, envy and competition.

We should be quick to counteract this false choice
with the idea that passions do indeed have a right to
a political citizenship that is not simply instrumental.
We need critical projects to be built that take as their
guarantee, against excessive narcissism, the motor of
those shared passions that respect democratic ideals
and confront the neoliberal model. A new government

of the passions must proceed by way of a constant coupling of *attention* with a certain type of *methodological decentring*.

What we are proposing is not an act of reflection: if that were the case, then paying attention to the passions would mean subjecting them to the umpteenth government of reason. Nor is this an effort to shift passions from the realm of the unconscious to the realm of the conscious. Rather we could define *attention as a passion for one's own passions*. This means working *with* the passions to make them active subjects (to transform them into *affects*, some would say), to use them as symptoms of what motivates or drives us to political engagement, and to admit with honesty which passions predominate, what type of mix works for us, and to what extent these passions are permanent dispositions of our very character (and thus combine to make us virtuous) and are consistent with the political goals and values we want to head towards.

This attention towards our own passions, typical of self-government, must, however, be accompanied by a constant effort at *methodological decentring*. We could almost say that a politician (and not only a politician but anyone who happens to exercise a position of power) would benefit from the habit of exercising a healthy *scepticism* about her own role; of paying attention to her own passions, so that she may not be fixed to the centre of the political stage and thus may be able to understand better the consequences of her actions. This methodological shift means breaking out of the individualising effect of leaderism, through which the discussion of *politics* has become today, almost invariably, a discussion of *politicians*.[21] For this reason it can be a genuine political method, which breaks away from mechanisms by now worn out. For instance this mechanism: every time a new election is on the horizon (and nowadays there is *always* an election coming up!), people get excited and the same old script starts playing out: there is an appeal, then there is a response, then the political discussion heats up *exclusively* around the question of the names of candidates and who should choose them. When the moment comes, an election campaign is conducted in which all split up again, promoting their own candidate against the others, even though they have signed up to the same appeal and the same programme. Finally, our lives remain just the same. Our political passions are all dominated by identification with a single individual (a 'dictatorship resting on the exploitation of mass emotionality', as Weber put it).[22] Our choices are limited to personal sympathy or antipathy.

Above all, this script is out of date. For it probably belongs to those times when representation was clearer: the social classes had not decomposed, the party system responded to unmistakable ideal visions, and the politician's personal touch really could indeed make a difference – but within an ideologically entrenched perimeter. To delude ourselves that *anyone* could come along to unite what contemporary capitalism has divided is to fail to understand that the attack has targeted that entrenched perimeter: an idea of society, the very capacity to bring passions together without their being measured by the yardstick of a blind individualism. This is why we ought to seek by all means to value those passions that are useful to decentring.

This preoccupation with a pathological passion for

self-recognition is also shared by the very people to whom it refers. It is another passional mechanism of a projective nature (actually this one is not restricted to the political sphere), which we could define in the following terms: for many people, the ego clearly benefits from a state of exception. We can explain this with the help of a concrete example. A professor who had held power in the university for decades once attempted to persuade everyone to vote for him again. He used more or less this argument: 'The university has been in crisis for decades. Who can help save it better than me, when I know the place and have run it for decades?' We get the same thing in politics, too. Each person recognises the limitations, shares a cutting analysis, and calls for the renewal of people and practices. He takes the floor, shouting that it is necessary to 'make way for new approaches'. But it is always he who takes the floor, is interviewed, introduces and concludes our meetings, takes it upon himself to make the important decisions. Self-centredness reaches its most extreme point: the ego is protected by the fact of being in a state of exception vis-à-vis the world that it judges. Now it is no longer of this world.

It is not difficult to find these same dynamics and these same passions when we look at the factors behind the partial decline of the myth of participatory democracy. For at least a decade, this myth has led us to call for civil society's aid in expanding the channels of representation.

In certain regards, this political concentration on what might allow for greater participation has produced irreversible positive effects in terms of innovation and extension of the regulating idea of equality. And yet the paradigm of participation probably did not live up to what it promised, especially if we consider a critical function able to rethink thoroughly the relational mechanisms of political practice. At least until now, it has not proved itself all that able to change and renew decision-making processes or to initiate a more dynamic relationship between the governing and the governed. As for the mobilisation of passions, its emotional failure is often none too distant from the similar failure of representative democracy. So-called civil society too often appears to be in the same position: an unrelenting and uninhibited leaderism (how many associations are based on a monarchical cult of a leader?); dynamics of leadership groups whose passion for power – even a scrap of it – destroys any idealistic dedication; connivance with politics that frequently imposes a rather suspicious silence in exchange for little attention; and a hypertrophy of recognition. If, disappointed by her experience of politics, the young girl from Vinca decided instead to participate in a meeting of one of the many local associations, she would probably find the same dynamics. This mimicry confirms how far neoliberalism's contamination of the passions has poisoned even those spaces that ought to constitute bastions of opposition. But we need to make a brief detour into the political effects of this contamination of the passions.

In our view, there is one prevalent passion that has altered the possible relationship between widened participation and the effectiveness of representation. And this passion is mistrust. In one of the most celebrated analyses of recent years, Rosanvallon defines the main tendency under way in western democracies thus: 'democracy of distrust'.[23] Although he recognises the risks that this entails, the French scholar is inspired by a certain optimism. In his judgement, mistrust contributes to a rearrangement of representation beyond its permanent crisis, triggering mechanisms of participatory control that – to use our earlier categories – permit greater legitimacy for the governing and greater powers of surveillance for the governed. This is not all wrong. Citizens' participatory activity remains an irreplaceable tool, which permits proactive control of the mechanisms of representation and raises the overall quality of democracy.

However, Rosanvallon's interpretation seems to go only so far in taking heed of the fact that distrust is a passion and, as such, permanently shapes the very structure of the social bond. It is a passion that concerns our relations with others; but it is not a joyous passion, let alone a shared one. It is not a joyous passion because it is led by suspicion or hostility; and it is not a shared passion because, seen through mistrustful eyes, democracy is a place where threat is always possible – and certainly not a place of potential improvement to our existence. If we look closely at how distrust operates in the interaction between representation and participation, we will find much more confirmation for these risks than for the hopes raised by Rosanvallon.

The most visible consequence of a democracy of distrust is the refusal of any proxy, even when the distance from representatives is diminished through some kind of internal democracy or through the enactment of participatory processes. The call for transparency (or the suspicion it projects) ends up paralysing any capacity to make decisions. For the passional alter ego of distrust is a passion we have met already: vanity, or an unquenchable desire for recognition that – with an entirely symbolic tenacity – goes as far as to contest any decision enacted on our behalf, simply because someone else has taken it. Distrust becomes the weapon of a dogged but puny defence of one's grandiose self. It reveals a stubbornly anti-political passion: one in which the ego is prepared to be governed only by itself – which is also the only self that can govern others, since the ego is a state of exception. Thus any experience of participation is reduced to a constant complaint, directed not only at fundamental choices but also at trivial things – the form of words chosen in a press release or the order in which speakers should intervene at a conference. Even as these trifles become the symbolic pretexts through which they can assert their exclusive right to decide for themselves, the essential decisions are taken elsewhere. Participation is literally taken prisoner, annulled by this passion that pulls apart what is held in common rather than working to find innovative patterns.

Here it is none too difficult to see at work a non-constructive coupling of passions: *a blend of distrust and vanity* that makes participation almost pointless from a political point of view. It does not seem a good idea to have transformed every individual citizen into a *master of suspicion*.

The analogy between the use of passions in the spaces of representation and their use at the site of participation thus proves far from being ill ventured. We can even unpack the same question: What political use does participation actually have? If its purpose is a struggle for the exclusive recognition of the ideas of which I am the proprietor, it will contribute far more to undoing democracy than to reimagining it.

After all, in the original idea of representation – that is, in the tension that results from the fact that the governing cannot entirely coincide with the governed, even though the only possible legitimation comes from the latter – there is more than an implicit admission of the need that some exert power over others. There is also a golden rule regarding the way in which passions are to be used in politics: they may be the passions of the many or the few, but they should never coincide with the passions of one person against everyone else. In the vulnerable and noble idea of representation there is an emotional intelligence that suggests that agreement (and disagreement) be built on those passions that are able to mobilise us together. Precisely because of its imperfect capacity to keep the governing tied to the governed, representation stands opposed to any appropriation. It calls for inclusive, not for exclusive passions – for a construction of political links that should be able to combine my readiness to allow that another represent me with care to make sure that this is done the right way (and also at the other end: readiness to represent others, and care to make sure that this representation is realised). Only this tenacious construction can transform individual malaise into a political conflict. Yet we get instead the sensation that, even in the play of present-day democracy, all we can be is proprietors or consumers – as Hirschman already observed in his own way;[24] or in any case that we are unable to have *certain* shared passions. All that remains, then, would be to govern in the name of others as if they could not think differently from me, since I perceive myself to be the owner of an entire political culture – to the point of requiring charismatic identification in the leader as a unique gesture of political freedom; or to exercise, on those who govern, the same control and suspicion as would a consumer who demands neither more or less than a private law contract: it is individualised and connected to something that concerns me only because it belongs to me.

Conclusions

In his essay *Learning Democracy*, Gustavo Zagrebelsky offered a short but profound piece of reflection on one of the great pedagogical questions raised in all modern democracies.[25] Is it possible, the author asked, 'to teach, not democracy, but the act of *subscribing to democracy?*' In other words, can we reasonably assume that 'it is possible to teach not *what democracy is*, but what it is *to be democrats*, to embrace democracy as an ideal in one's own conduct, as a virtue to honour and translate into practice?'[26]

The updated response, one decade on, is in some regards a paradoxical one. It would be very difficult to continue to believe that our democracy can resolve the multiple problems in its functioning – from the institutional order to the displacement of sovereignty, from subordination to economic government to the oligarchical tendency of producing a dizzying rise in inequalities – if it continues to underestimate the role of the passions in the disappointed experience of representation and participation. We need more than ever to return to a republican pedagogy that should able to teach us to be democrats before anything else.

A legitimate withdrawal from the customary sites of democracy has already taken place. This is more than confirmation of a contest that the democratic ideal is losing. Perhaps it also marks other fields of resistance that are emerging, people who are trying to *be democrats* even though democracy has left them at the margins.

Even disengagement – which seems to be the main cipher for many people's public identity – can be observed with other feelings than worry. It also represents a paradoxical act of disobedience vis-à-vis a system led by neoliberal passions, by the logic of competition and survival of the fittest. It is a disengagement that shows a form of passive resistance.

It is not a given that this disengagement must be the only solution left. Of course, a relentless deconstruction of power that aims to recognise it as the force that imposes a certain style of government over our lives is already a return to a critical labour on politics. We should remember Foucault's humble advice that the only authentically possible critique is 'the art of not being governed quite so much'.[27]

In any case, we can no longer think of politics as a redemption mechanism. A mobilisation founded on critical analyses and systematic responses that are really up to task – and not just on electoral calculations – is all the more necessary as it is forbidden by the indiscriminate use of the passions imposed by neoliberalism, a use that represents one of the instruments designed to frustrate any credible alternative project. For this reason we need to habituate ourselves to real exercises of critical treatment of the everyday, which should deprive power of the possibility to decide what *form* our lives take – and not only what *contents* they have – and should restore to each person the possibility of debating in public not so much what we are allowed to be, but rather what we feel and what we *want* to be. Paying detailed, programmatic attention to the passions that circulate among us is a formidable tool for learning how *to be democrats* again.

In this chapter we have simply described an *unhealthy affectivity*, the kind of government of the passions that *contaminates* our politics – but also our workplaces, our family relations, our strenuous relationship with desires and their colonisation; and, quite often, it also annihilates the building of those small groups we started out from. In all these experiences, the unhealthy affectivity accompanies the small everyday resistances of the generations who do not give in to the conformism of passions, of values, of languages; who carry out acts of pure generosity, who leave their behaviours free of the need for consumption, who 'waste time' in search of beauty and not profit, who build communities and connections, continuing to call for democracy.[28] All this was also open to many generations in the past. But they did not have to do it *against politics*, like today.

As we will attempt to demonstrate, the family is a specific field, able to shape our relationship with our passions. The contest between the dominion of neoliberal passions and an education in inclusive passions is playing out also within our family relations. And it is these inclusive passions that are able to push us away from the conviction that everything we experience must necessarily have that 'fixed smile [that] nevertheless has the impermanent quality of something stamped into uncooperative material'.[29]

Shifting attention towards certain experiences of

private life could help politics either by evoking another affective order within political language or by reacting through a real *political pedagogy* to neoliberalism's check on the governance of our emotions.

4
Familial Passions and the Passion for the State

Familial love

On no other terrain are passions so intense as in the family. Families are the privileged site of emotions and affects, intimacy and dependency, love and hate, an extraordinary centre of formation, socialisation and the construction of opinion. The family's outlook is characterised by a twofold perspective: one is intimate, the other focused on the outside world, and the latter is of greater concern to us here. It is no exaggeration to say that families are the protagonists of everyday politics, in large measure defining individuals' approach to the rest of the world. For Gramsci, families were, at least potentially, 'organs of moral life'.[1] As such, they are of immense interest for our purposes.

Political theory long tended to ignore families, relegating them to the background, starved of analytical attention. But this neglect does not reflect their real importance. Today's public opinion surveys repeatedly show the predominance of the family in everyday life. In the 2008 European Values Survey that sought to establish the importance of the family in European citizens' lives, 86% of those interviewed answered that they considered it 'very important', figures reaching 96% in Turkey and Iceland (an unlikely but suggestive pairing). The lowest percentage was in Sweden (55%).[2]

Love, compassion, care – above all across different generations and from one gender (female) to another (male) – and the readiness to make sacrifices (this, too, has gender connotations in a large part), all stand out on our list of familial passions. In a religious context, and not only Catholicism, family virtues are very much foregrounded. For the nineteenth-century Catholic philosopher Antonio Rosmini, the family was 'almost a little church within the walls of the home'.[3] But this approach also presents certain risks, insofar as it makes excessive demands on the family, imposing impossible standards and strongly idealised models.

In the rebirth of social thinking in Great Britain that came with, and informed, the creation of the welfare state after the end of the Second World War, the psychoanalyst Donald Winnicott chose a different approach. He extolled the virtues of what he characterised as the 'normal' or 'good enough family' ('the family that is more or less up to task') in the sense that, while it can never be perfect, it is nonetheless able to deal with the many demands and passions of everyday life.[4] For Winnicott, 'normality' was the objective that families tirelessly worked towards, after the devastating experience of two world wars in barely three decades. It was the hope that the family would finally be able to live and reproduce itself in peace, in a 'propitious' environment, particularly suited to the needs of mothers and newborns. For Winnicott, if 'normal, good' family units were tied to the welfare state, they would be a fertile terrain for democracy.

In any case, here as in other sections of this book we need to proceed with circumspection. Families can be sites of great harmony, but also a living hell. From a historical perspective, the weaker members of the family unit – young women and children, the elderly and the sick – have usually been the object of cruelty, physical violence and neglect from male heads of household, often with the aid and complicity of the oldest female figure. It is no coincidence that, as Pushkin observed, the chants traditionally sung at weddings in the Russian countryside in the early nineteenth century resembled dirges at funerals more than festive hymns.[5]

You cannot escape the family. We can make more and more choices in our lives, but we cannot pick our parents. The writer and poet Dodie Smith suggests a tempered version of these passions. In 1938 she wrote: 'The family – that dear octopus from whose tentacles we never quite escape, nor, in our inmost hearts, ever quite wish to.'[6] But there are many other narratives, and rather more bitter ones.

Besides, families can be the site of the worst suspicion, intrigue and selfishness. In 1936 François Mauriac, who would win the Nobel Prize for Literature sixteen years later, published his famous novel *The Knot of Vipers*, whose subject was family life in provincial France. Present therein were all the sad passions – greed and meanness, pride and hatred, the desire to dominate, and the list goes on.

When we talk about the passions of the family, there are a lot of different fields to investigate. A first distinction, which we already mentioned at the beginning of this chapter, is the one between passions *internal* to the family and passions *external* to it. Here we will concentrate on the latter, which are more germane to the political inquiry at the centre of the present volume. What aspect does familial virtue assume in the contemporary world? In what relation with the public sphere do familial passions stand – especially the love of the family? What risk is there that the state's interests will be subordinated to the private needs and passions of the family? We want to sketch out a response to these interlinked questions with reference to three rather different fields of enquiry: the reflections developed in ancient Greece and in Chinese communism and Confucianism, and the challenges encountered by Italian families in the republican era.

Antiquity

The very existence of the family and its difficulty in expressing virtue were the object of a much more animated debate in ancient Greece than in our own time. In the *Republic*, Plato expresses a deep scepticism with regard to the ability of the guardians in Callipolis to act as spokesmen for its interests and for those of their respective families at the same time. To resolve this problem, he proposes the abolition both of private property and of families for the guardians. Only on that condition, claimed Plato, would they remain true defenders of the city; only then would it be possible to

> prevent them from distracting the city by referring 'mine' not to the same but to different things, one man dragging off to his own house anything he is able to acquire

apart from the rest and another doing the same to his own separate house, and having women and children apart, thus introducing into the state the pleasures and pains of individuals.[7]

This famous portrayal of the relations between the family and the republic left very little space for compromise. One's 'own' and the privacy of family life were considered potentially ruinous for politics in the ideal city-state and for *virtue*. Later on the Greek Stoics would assume a similar position, in fact an even more radical one: equal dignity ought to be bestowed on all human beings. They were not citizens of a specific city-state (and in this the Stoics' vision differed from Plato's) or members of families, but *kosmopolitai*, members of the 'city-state of the universe'.[8] Love for their own families or grief for their deaths thus had no space in the Stoics' hierarchy of the passions. On the contrary, families fomented jealousy and rivalry. It was better that children be raised by the community and that parental roles do not exist.

For Aristotle, on the contrary, the sense of 'mine' expressed in the family and in the individual domestic unit was exactly the essence the *polis* was built upon. In the *Politics* he energetically challenges Plato's ideas, arguing that they would entail the destruction of the state and of those affective ties of blood on which the growth of the future generations depended: 'a state essentially consists of a multitude of persons',[9] he wrote, and as such it depended on individual families, each endowed with a house and property. For Aristotle, real kinship based on individual families was infinitely preferable to community ties, as we can deduce from his clear statement that 'it is better for a boy to be one's own private nephew than one's son in the way described' (i.e. on the Platonic model).[10]

Yet it is crucial for our purposes to note that Aristotle did not stop here. He was very far from a supine acceptance of the status quo of Greek families of his day. On the contrary, in the *Politics* he calls for a whole series of measures with a view to transforming the family: it was necessary to encourage men and boys to eat their meals together by organising public dining halls (*syssitia*) – and not on a limited scale, only for certain categories of citizens such as the magistrates and the priests, but for all male citizens.[11] None of the citizens should have excessive or insufficient property, for 'surely the ideal of the state is to consist as much as possible of persons who are equal and alike'.[12] Education from the age of seven on should be the responsibility not of the family but of the state. Commenting on this proposal, Aristotle drew close to Plato (at least to his *Laws*, if not to the *Republic*):

> And inasmuch as the end for the whole state is one, it is manifest that education also must necessarily be one and the same for all and that the superintendence of this must be public, and not on private lines, in the way in which at present each man superintends the education of his own children, teaching them privately, and whatever special branch of knowledge he thinks fit.[13]

We should always bear in mind that Aristotle's concept of *polis*, which qualifies these views, was based on important elements of exclusion, in particular concerning women and slaves. For both Aristotle and Plato, citizenship was a highly selective category. Aristotle's observations nonetheless continue to have considerable resonance in our own world, and his proposals – which do not go as far as to invoke the abolition of the family or of private property – still have a surprisingly radical tone even today. It is good to ask ourselves what the modern equivalent of the *syssitia*, the public dining halls, might be, and what families could share among themselves. It seems that the passion for sharing among families, to which we will return, reached much greater levels of intensity in ancient Greece than in the opulent consumerism of the contemporary age.

Confucianism and Chinese communism

Thus far we have focused our attention especially on the debate regarding the very existence of the family and its individual dimension. While Plato and Aristotle started out from diametrically opposed positions, they each emphasised the need to integrate the family into the state, limiting its autonomy in order to guarantee its continued survival. But in another ancient culture – Chinese Confusianism – the outlook was very different. Obviously Confusianism was not the only moral doctrine present in China, nor was China the only Asian territory in which Confucius' teaching spread its influence. But perhaps we would not go too far from the truth by emphasising what is of particular interest for our purposes, namely that in Confucianism the family itself constitutes the object of the dominant passions. Given the extraordinary importance that China has assumed in the modern world, this deep-rooted passion is worthy of further study.

At the centre of Confucianism, in the version offered by Mencius (ca. 372–289 BC), five main relations are linked together: the love between father and son, the loyalty between king and minister, the distinction between husband and wife, the precedence of the old over the young man, and good faith between friends. This hierarchically ordered set of relations necessarily demands immediate reflection. First of all, it is clear that the father–son relationship, which is founded on filial piety (*hsiao*), is the only one explicitly attributed the status of *love*, and as such dominates Confucianism's moral doctrine. Second, a strong gender connotation is in evidence: women appear in fact only as a secondary element in the third relationship listed, the one between husband and wife – and, even then, only to establish the 'difference' between the sexes' respective responsibilities in the household. Lastly, family relations are predominant both numerically and in order of importance. The family (*jia*) reigns supreme.[14]

Mencius himself summarised admirably this hierarchy of affects: 'A wise man loves his parents but is merely benevolent towards the people; *he is benevolent towards the people but is merely sparing with animals.*' '(Throughout this passage Mencius is exploiting the fact that the word *ai* means both "to love" and "to be sparing, to be frugal".)'[15]

Examining Confucianism's ideal family in detail, we find one striking further element, which corresponds directly to passions. Loyalty to the family is inflected not only with reference to the present but also with reference to the distant past. Children honour the souls of their parents, keeping the lineage alive across generations of ancestors. Hence, if it is the family that sparks an undying passion, this is a particular kind of family: one that extends across an infinite arc of time, beyond physical death.

In the presence of such families and family traditions, there was inevitably an ongoing battle to guarantee family loyalty to the state. Francis Fukuyama has referred to the traditions of classical Chinese drama, which would often portray the torments of a son forced to choose between loyalty to his own family and obedience to the state. In one drama, Confucius enters into confrontation with the sovereign of a bordering state. Once again, the discussion centres on the nature of virtue:

> The king boasted to Confucius that virtue in his land was such that if a father stole, his son would report the crime and the criminal to the state. Confucius replied that in his state virtue was far greater, for a son would never think of treating his father so.[16]

The governing elites represented Chinese society as a large family, with the emperor in the role of supreme patriarch. But, with the weakening of the imperial state, nepotism and clan power raged uncontrolled. Olga Lang has offered a powerful description of this phenomenon for the period 1935–7.[17] In such circumstances the individual and proprietary passions identified by Hobbes had free rein. Even the solution offered by Chinese history was Hobbesian in character. After a very violent civil war (followed in turn by a Japanese invasion), the Chinese Communist Party (CCP) imposed its iron fist.

After the CCP took power in 1949, the traditional primacy of devotion to the Confucian family inevitably had to give way to communist ideology. The new state, which based its own power on the solid pillars of the party and the army, undertook important initiatives to encourage the emancipation of women, both within and outside the family. In his famous *Report on an*

Investigation of the Peasant Movement in Hunan in March 1927, Mao Zedong very eloquently analysed the shackles that weighed down the population (80% of it were peasants) and from which the communists intended to liberate it.

> A man in China is usually subjected to the domination of three systems of authority: (1) the state system (political authority), ranging from the national, provincial and county government down to that of the township; (2) the den system (clan authority), ranging from the central ancestral temple and its branch temples down to the head of the household; and (3) the supernatural system (religious authority) [...]. As for women, in addition to being dominated by these three systems of authority, they are also dominated by the men (the authority of the husband). These four authorities – political, clan, religious and masculine – are the embodiment of the whole feudal–patriarchal system and ideology, and are the four thick ropes binding the Chinese people, particularly the peasants.[18]

The new regime worked to limit the influence of the traditional patrilineal and patrilocal family despite the constant resistance it met, especially in the countryside. The 1950 law on marriage and the campaign to put it into effect from 1950 to 1953 saw the peak of the new regime's mobilisation around family themes.[19] Like the other great tyrannies of the twentieth century, the communist regime established a direct link with the new generations. School provided for both education (we need only think of the fight against rural illiteracy) and indoctrination. Particularly controversial were the measures that attempted to overcome the demographic situation of the time. Directly challenging the Confucian stipulation that families should produce many male off-spring, these measures allowed now just one single heir per family. Couples expressed a strong preference for males, and secret female infanticide became the norm on a vast scale.[20]

The first three decades of communist rule, from 1949 to 1978, were marked by an enormous loss of human life. We cannot enter into the details of these terrible events here, and we do not need to. But it is worth remembering that Mao's Great Leap Forward policy of 1958–9, which imposed the collectivisation of agriculture and the relocation of peasants in enormous production communes, would lead to an unprecedented famine in 1959–62, especially in the Henan, Anhui, Shandong and Sichuan provinces. It is impossible to obtain secure figures regarding the number of families destroyed; we can only say that the deaths were in the tens of millions.[21]

As for the relations between family and state, the specific object of our interest, the Great Leap Forward and the famine that followed were the most dramatic twentieth-century example of disruptive economic and political interventions, made without any proper con-sideration of the possible social consequences. In China in the late 1950s, some of the most negative political passions in our vocabulary entered the fray: the armed narcissism that stubbornly leads humanity along the path to disaster, the falseness of the programmatic promises made to the peasants, and the cynicism of an elite inured to countless horrors and now prepared to play around with the population's fate.

This history has an extraordinary finale. When the long wave of Maoism finally waned and Deng Xiaoping took power in 1978, the country was swept by a new wind of autonomous enterprise and individual economic growth. With a deft ideological leap, Deng introduced the 'theory of the cat': what matters is not the colour of the cat, but that it should catch the mouse – in this case, economic progress. For the first time, the peasants were granted ownership of the pieces of land they worked themselves. Small businesses were strongly encouraged.[22]

Concurrently, powerful elements of the old Confucian family culture and other familiar kinds of reverence for the family resurfaced. In 2012 the demographic restrictions were considerably relaxed. Families had regained power and influence, and the very essence of the communist regime risked being undermined from within, as family interests and the pursuit of individual wealth took priority. Far from following the model of Plato's guardians, the political leaders became champions of their own families. One of the most dramatic examples of this transformation concerns Wen Jiabao and his relatives. Wen was prime minister from 2003 to 2013, and during that period his family accumulated a fortune estimated at $2.7 billion. This new wealth was administered by his son, his daughter, his younger brother and his brother-in-law. Wen's wife Zhang Beili was well known among the Chinese élite because she controlled the country's trade in jewels and precious stones.[23]

What does all this tell us about passions, families and states? First, it teaches us that family love, one of the deepest human emotions, does not automatically express 'virtue'. Virtue is achieved only when family love is accompanied by a deep perceptiveness and a sense of the need to protect what belongs to the public sphere. *Public goods* – be they a public hospital ward for premature babies, the water that comes out of a kitchen tap, or the large city park donated to the state – are necessarily an object of public care and affection. *The balance and interaction between these two types – family love and collective love – are decisive for modern politics.* It seems that Aristotle deeply understood this: individual families make up the state, but they give it form only if they are intimately and constantly connected to the public sphere. The great philosopher wrote that 'mine' 'is the very essence on which the *polis* is built'.

The Chinese case is highly instructive; for it invites us to look beyond the surface level of contemporary politics and recognise the extraordinary power of the longue durée, of deeply rooted credos and values that are able to flourish once more after decades of repression and indoctrination. Wen Jiabao was undoubtedly a good communist in the Chinese sense of the term, officially dedicated to the service of the Chinese state. But he was also married to Zhang Beili and passionately served his own family, accumulating material goods on a vast scale. His was an unhealthy affectivity, which derived from an excess of love and ambition for a single family – his own.

Passions for the family and the failure of republican pedagogy in Italy

The question of unhealthy affectivities deserves further attention, this time with specific reference to contemporary Italy. The emotion itself – love for a daughter or a son, or for an entire family unit – is not at all *unhealthy*. What is unhealthy is the nature and scope of the field in which it appears and of the praxes it adopts, which amount to an instrumental use of public posts and resources for the sake of satisfying desires and passions related to one's own family. How many politicians, professionals and other ruling-class figures have taken this path in Italy, without the slightest sense of self-critique and without ever being called on to explain their behaviour? When this does happen, they tend to make excuses for themselves, just as Bettino Craxi did before the Chamber of Deputies on 3 July 1992. Accused of having violated the law on party funding, he replied that it was well known that illegal financing was an essential part of the Italian political system, and as such should be accepted. This was the classic excuse: 'if everyone is doing it, why can't I?' The more the politicians turn a blind eye to wrongdoing – or even go so far as to argue that it is functional for the system – the smaller the chance that republican pedagogy (at all age levels) would prosper.

As we analyse unhealthy affectivities in Italy, we absolutely need to reflect on the enduring importance of familism and clientelism. Modern familism is a distorted *relationship* between individuals, families, civil society and the state in which families unduly and even exclusively concentrate on themselves and devote a minimal proportion of their time to civil society and to the state.[24] In 1958 the US sociologist Edward Banfield coined the expression 'amoral familism' to refer to the behaviour of the inhabitants of Chiaromonte, a small town in Basilicata to which he gave the imaginary name 'Montegrano' in order to maintain the anonymity of its inhabitants. For Banfield, the extreme backwardness of

Montegrano was due to 'the inability of the villagers to act together for their common good or, indeed, for any end transcending the immediate, material interest of the nuclear family'.[25] Many Italian commentators have expressed their conviction that the economic transformations that took place in those years, from mass migration to rapid industrialisation, marked the end of such 'archaic' familism. But that was not at all the case. A whole series of factors – the lack of a republican pedagogy to teach an alternative vision of the relationship between love for the family and love for the state, the lack of political sensitivity to the importance of this problem, the porous nature of the state itself, and above all an inability to invest in collective solutions – allowed familism the space it needed to breed and flourish.

The same argument largely applies to clientelism as well. Historically, clientelism took the form of a dyadic relationship between patron and client in which the client pledged loyalty to the patron in exchange for respect, services and material benefits. Referring to contemporary Italy, the anthropologist Amalia Signorelli has proposed the following definition of clientelism:

> A system of interpersonal relations in which private relations of parental, ritual–parental, and friendly type are effective within public structures, so as to realise a use of public resources that is advantageous in private terms.[26]

Here we are very close to that unhealthy affectivity, which considers the public sphere a terrain to be plundered rather than a source of collective benefits. Those who put themselves at the service of patrons – often for want of alternatives – must necessarily behave like those Machiavellian monkeys who made their appearance in chapter 3. But we should note that clientelism is home not only to servility but also to one of the most heartfelt passions: loyalty. It was Leopoldo Franchetti, in his famous study on late-nineteenth-century Sicilian politics and society, who observed that patron–client relations could inspire a devotion 'that knows neither limits nor scruples nor remorse'.[27] Such is the basis on which the various mafias have built their fortunes.

This would seem to be the exact opposite of an effective republican pedagogy or, to return to ancient Greece for a moment, of the sophist Protagoras' convinced response to Socrates on the subject of the capacity of society and family to inculcate 'virtue':

> They teach and admonish [their children] from earliest childhood till the last day of their lives. As soon as one of them grasps what is said to him, the nurse, the mother, the tutor, and the father himself strive hard that the child may excel, and as each act and word occurs they teach and impress upon him that this is just, and that unjust, one thing noble, another base, one holy, another unholy, and that he is to do this, and not do that.[28]

The set of emotions and actions that we can identify across Europe, and especially in the biggest urban agglomerations, is utterly different. Parents face increasing difficulties in raising their children and often delegate their responsibilities of care and instruction to underpaid and demoralised teachers. Only very recently, the head of a primary school in Darlington, in the north of England, wrote to the children's parents begging them at least to dress properly for taking their children to school and not to turn up wearing pyjamas and slippers under a coat.[29] It remains to be seen

Passions for the family

whether Winnicott's 'good enough' families are really good enough today.

Since 2008, families have been victim to growing tensions. The protracted global crisis has demonstrated neoliberalism's vulnerability both as an economic philosophy and as a cultural model. In Italy the gradual aggravation of the crisis has corresponded to the intensification of car adverts on television. The year 2015 saw the slogan 'Alfa Romeo, *the mechanics of the emotions*', coined in order to advertise the company's new Giulia model. But families do register the obvious injustice inherent in bailing out the banks, the astronomical rise in inequalities, and the sharp cuts in all aspects of the welfare state. The hopes associated with 'normality' vanished with the erosion of families' savings; and family units often managed to survive only thanks to the modest pensions of the elderly.

In such a moment the historical, deep-rooted distortions represented by clientelism and familism have come to exert, again, an ever more intense influence on the Italian republic, particularly in the domain of youth unemployment. Far from disappearing, these social mechanisms have become stronger amid the general crisis of neoliberal economics. Whom you know, who you are, what family you come from, with what recommendations and through what channels you arrive, are all factors able to bear decisive influence in a labour market that is shamelessly oriented towards employers' interests.

In some Italian regions, and not only in the south, the way out is to join a criminal clan: a means of gaining rapid access to certain types of job, to money, and to local influence. But the human costs are very high and distance us from the passions that are at the basis of this book.

In reverse

Up until now, the passions of the family and the passion for the state have been described in a manner that brought out the great distance between them. We have thus given a sort of predominance to the unhealthy affectivity expressed in the primitive form of illicit enrichment of the family unit at the expense of the state. Yet this is not *necessarily* the only possible outcome. Once we manage to identify and analyse the countervailing passions and motives, the path that takes us back to a more civil and fairer system suddenly takes a clear shape. Spaces then open up for alternatives, for lively debates, for first initiatives and proposals from small groups such as that of the teenagers with whom we exchanged – sadly – only a few words in Vinca that afternoon. Once they have been created, the virtuous circles develop extraordinarily quickly – especially today – and the same applies to the ideas and proposals they entail. But it should also be said that the circles of civil society can easily become demoralised.

It does not take much for selfishness, untrammelled ambition, disorganised meetings, the so-called flamers who spew bile on web forums to destroy an initiative in the space of a few months – or a few years at most. Self-discipline, the ability to listen, the respectful use of time (above all, that of others), patience allied with determination, serious attention to the form as well as the content of meetings, and especially the deployment of shared passions have an extraordinary capacity to rock the boat. The inclusive passions that this book has described are 'dangerous' for the self-centred elites of the public sphere, for they promise to spark a dynamic in which families and the democratic state come closer to each other.

When we think about the passions that drive people into action, we would like to point out especially *curiosity* as a possible characteristic of families' new conduct – alongside respect for *privacy*. So let us start from another paradox; for at first glance curiosity may seem to be the enemy of privacy. In the debate on passions that took place in the seventeenth century, two female characters – Eve and Pandora – were summoned to represent curiosity. As we know, in both cases curiosity had disastrous consequences. But Hobbes took its side. In his view curiosity, unlike passions such as joy and sadness, was something exclusive to human beings. He considered it a mobilising passion, which pushed people to break out of their lethargy, in search for new explanations of everything around them.[30] In modern terms, curiosity functions as an incentive to action. It prompts us to single out differences and to want to understand them; and it draws us closer to the world's great problems. But we also need to know how to guard against an excess of curiosity. The history of the twentieth century bears witness to the oppressive invasion of the private family by the great tyrannical states. Curiosity and privacy may very well follow different paths, but when they are combined they are an enormous stimulus for families to act, to get out of the house – and today they do so in the knowledge that they will be able to return home. We are very far from the hyperactivity of civil society under Russian and Chinese communism, which sought to make serving the tyrannical state the apex of public passion.

A second important line of thought concerns the characteristics of the associations open to families or individuals. Robert Putnam has suggested a first distinction between 'bridging' (or inclusive) and 'bonding' (or exclusive) groups.[31] In the first case, we are close to common passions and groups that tend to promote wider identities and reciprocities; in bonding groups, instead, specific interests and passions are favoured, with the latent risk that one group's identity will be asserted at the expense of others.

Obviously, these are not ironclad categories; indeed, we have already had reason to note that the definition a group gives of itself may stand totally at odds with the actual practices of its adherents. But for us, armed as we are with a healthy sense of suspicion, it is bridging groups that are particularly of interest. The families that have greater propensity for openness than for closedness, show empathy with other families, and express concerns in front of the great and pressing problems that afflict the contemporary world have a pressing need for inclusive groups: these will prevent them from being swamped by the isolation they are pitched into and will make sure that their good intentions are not frustrated.

One last consideration concerns the relationship we can detect between passions that are 'internal' and passions that are 'external' to families, which – we should be clear – are not necessarily the same ones. There may be an affectionate, joyous and paritary attitude *within* the family, which does not, however, prevent it from being ill informed and indifferent – or lacking in curiosity – with regard to the world *around*. Indeed, faced with the worsening global situation, families react by covering their eyes, the better to maintain their own internal sense of security and affection. Humans have an extremely powerful capacity to deny reality.

The changes effected by more than thirty-five years of neoliberalism have done very little to make families feel more connected. On the contrary, neoliberal romanticism is oriented towards seducing and distracting them, towards presenting Alfa Romeo's 'mechanics of the emotions' as a surrogate for emotions themselves. Some mechanisms of the modern world – 'work and spend' systems; the practice that leads us to fill up our 'free time' and family time with a whole series of other tasks weighing on the individual, who is often a part-time or precarious worker; the habit of collapsing in front of the TV in the evening; and the non-stop flow of advertising – are all powerful incentives for families to become passive and detached, and above all concentrated on themselves. No wonder that in 1987, in a now famous interview, Margaret Thatcher asserted:

> There's no such thing as society. There are individual men and women and there are families. And no government can do anything except through people, and people must look after themselves first.[32]

These enterprising individuals, hardened by competition and driven by greed, are at the centre of the neoliberal world.

Yet this is only a single and rather reductive version of the relationship between the passions internal and external to families. If they are to be able to align, the democratic state has to make a conscious intervention in support of external passions, of love for causes that go beyond the narrow family environment. This is not the 'nanny state' derided by Thatcher but rather a state able to create the necessary supporting conditions at every level, the 'facilitating environment' so dear to Winnicott and so necessary for the development of 'good enough families'. The more the state shows itself to be welcoming and encouraging, the less will families tend to close in on themselves. State and family thus establish a deep reciprocal relationship.

Conclusion

A hundred pages later, where have we got to? We have explored the fundamental thesis according to which we should analyse the connections between passions and politics instead of relegating each kind to its own separate sphere. This is an extremely fruitful exercise not only at the level of theory, but also at the level of political practice; it has an unexpected capacity to bring to the fore relations and languages, behaviours and meanings. The more we are able to devote a detailed and programmatic attention to the passions that circulate among us, the more likely we will be to build a democratic sphere that should be dignified (in the Weberian sense), effective and sustainable.

We should be clear that this is no simple task. We are not carefree butterfly chasers on a resplendent summer afternoon, looking to capture the best specimens for our collection. There is no clear hierarchy of passions for politics to adopt, so that the 'good' ones are at the top and the 'bad' ones at the bottom. Passions are ambivalent and liable to change; even their names change over time. Nonetheless, it is certainly possible to identify each one and to use them in the political field. The methodology we have suggested has shown the need to devise a system of combinations. For passions have more resonance and become more useful when they are associated, specifically and repeatedly, with other passions or with behaviours and states of mind that can in some way condition their use and the intention behind them.

A key combination among the ones we have suggested is the one between gentleness and steadfastness; another, which concerns the family, links curiosity to respect for privacy; yet another binds ambition – a political passion par excellence – to temperance. These combinations border on the paradoxical, because they bring together passions that, though seeming to stand in *contradiction*, in fact *reinforce* each another. This effort to combine passions may prove highly fruitful in the absence of any pretentions to completeness or to a definitive view.

Moreover, every era has redefined the political utility of passions according to its different contexts, its established values or its emergent claims. As we have amply demonstrated, some combinations of passions and behaviours would be totally out of place now. It is rather strange that today, in an era in which the control of passions makes a powerful contribution to the predominance of a seriously iniquitous system of values and social organisation, some passions are held up as absolutes whereas others are silenced and no one feels any need for a collective concern for their mastery, with the political consequences that flow from it.

So, unconvinced both by the indiscriminate enthusiasm displayed in front of passions and by the thesis that they should be sacrificed on the altar of Reason, we propose an 'alphabet of passions'. As always, we should start from ourselves. The objective of the *self-government* that we proposed in chapter 3 is to prepare us for engagement in the political world. But we need to engage in a completely different way, granting a great deal of attention to *form* as well as to *content*. This involves, in lay terms, the capacity to listen and not to drone on and on, always repeating ourselves; the capacity to develop our human talents alongside those of others, abstaining from endless competition; the capacity to recognise narcissism both within and outside ourselves, in full awareness of its potentially lethal effects if it is left unchecked.

The 'alphabet of passions' does not concern only self-government and its various ramifications. It also means learning to distinguish between passions, to understand their complexity and to encourage the use of those with the power to spark further actions. Inclusive passions make up perhaps the most valuable part of this alphabet. These passions and attitudes, so relevant in this historical moment, can have an active function in orienting other passions that we need in the face of the fading landscape of present-day democracy, such as indignation and even rage. Taken alone, indignation and rage are often impotent passions, destined to produce further frustrations or – as is often the case – to reduce our desire for common transformation into simple anxiety at the prospect of destruction, or into relentless suspicion.

It is high time that discussions of the passions become a stable part of the curriculum in republican schools, rather than being ignored, undervalued or instrumentalised. This would be a great step forward. We hope that

Conclusion

the analytical distinctions we have attempted to advance will contribute to the creation of an informed popular base.

We should also remember to do what our predecessors forgot to do – or perhaps never learned to do: namely to connect politics with the family sphere. As we come to the end of this book, it is worth reasserting that families are the privileged site of emotions and affects and an extraordinary arena of education, socialisation and opinion formation. We ignore them at our peril.

Postscript

It has now been more than two years since the first pub-
lication of the Italian version of *Passions and Politics*. In
that time, the context for a debate on the passions has
changed with extraordinary rapidity. The intertwining
of global economic crisis and mass emigration – which
obviously had various intensities and locations – has
reproduced a combination of passions and states of
mind that many political commentators and politicians
had dismissed a long time ago as having no resonance
with mainstream democratic politics. Yet as early as in
1974 Primo Levi asked us to remember that 'every age
has its fascism' and warned us to be alert to the many
forms it could take.[1]

Looking at Europe alone, the epicentres for the sub-
version of European democracy in the 1920s and 1930s
were first Rome and then Berlin. We had occasion to
underline the combination of passions and states of
mind in the Nazi *Volksgemeinschaft* (see pp. 37–8):
solidarity with the poor and unemployed, as expressed
through the Winter Relief Fund; compassion for the

German mothers and wives who mourned their sons or husbands killed in the First World War; and horror at the little that remained (if anything) of the families burned to death in the Allies' firebombing of major German cities. Yet, alongside these passions, Nazism prospered by defining and promoting devastatingly fierce passions based on exclusion, submission, deportation and liquidation. The *dualism* apparent here – caring for one's own while denying the humanity of the other – is dramatically relevant for the present period. One can answer it only by reasserting an unshakeable defence of human rights.

If Rome and Berlin were once the epicentres of this phenomenon, today the epicentres are Warsaw, Budapest and Bratislava. But there are significant minorities of neo-fascists and neo-Nazis in every European country. Their driving passions include anger, resentment and fear. CasaPound, based in Rome, is an excellent example.[2]

Not only the most extreme phenomena have used regressive passions. Even that strange political mix of leadership and demagogy called 'populism', which very often takes a parliamentary course, seems to fan the flames of ancestral passions. It also foments bitterness about forcibly abandoned consumer dreams and about family welfare, first limited and then lost during the great economic crisis from 2008 onwards. Certainly there are various different representations of populism; and, insofar as it mostly represents a *form* of the relationship between governing and governed, populism is not necessarily filled with the *content* of regressive passions. But there is no doubt that, especially in the tired and lacklustre democracies of the West, populism appears (with rare and fortunate exceptions) as a phenomenon that amplifies hostile passions. When it strengthens shared passions, it does so by searching for an external enemy or a scapegoat. In short, what we face here is not a minoritarian phenomenon but a tendency that already today appears suspiciously capable of altering the order of political priorities in our democracies. We note, in all these cases, a government of passions that runs against the one we have suggested in this volume. This is true not only in the sense that it uses passions to increase inequalities, detract value from democratic processes, and reduce the spaces in which politics still appears as a shared potential. It is true also insofar as this government of passions seems to have forbidden the political valorisation of a combination that, in reality, seems more and more necessary: that between empathy and the lucidity of intelligence. Without recourse to these two brakes, political passions appear to be dogmatically exposed – as if they had no need for public legitimation apart from being seen to flex their muscles. It is as if the processes of spectacularisation had finally made our political passions virtual, and thus had made us unable to imagine what their consequences might be for real life. The more the prevalent political passions appear in virtual contexts, the more they risk losing their grounding in humanity. Is a study of the relationship between passions and politics still useful in this context? Obviously, we would say yes. And we can try to summarise, through the following schema, the reasons why this is the case:

First and foremost, we think that all the political phenomena to which we have just referred are doing more than proposing again disturbing cultural models that history has already passed judgement on. Their historically more innovative character lies in the fact that they have emerged as part of that theory of society (and not simply of economics) called neoliberalism. There exists, so we argue, an ongoing marriage beween political romanticism, certain passions, and neoliberalism that is worthy of further investigation.

Nor should we forget that the contemporary political representation of passions is also a generalised reaction to neoliberalism's devastating social effects. In this scenario, neoliberalism adopts the typical passions of its own imaginary. Resentment, competition, a blind conviction that the only way to build a community is to build up some enemy to serve as a target of hate. We suffer the perverse effects of neoliberalism in our own lives, but we lay the blame on democracy, which neoliberalism can only accept in a severely reduced form. This is why the habitual political use of passions seems so dangerous: because it corresponds to a general feeling of dissatisfaction with the present state of things but does not project any other idea of society. It thus seems that we can only express dissatisfaction using the blunt weapons of frustration, while neoliberal romanticism dominates not only our reality, but also our dreams. This romanticism takes the form either of realism (in the sense that neoliberal passions are the only ones that seem able to move reality and give it meaning) or of utopianism (in the sense that even the vision of change is unable to break out of the neoliberal imaginary).

Second, if the present moment is as serious as it seems, it cannot be enough to call for emancipation with the blunt weapons of political realism. If, to use Gramsci's famous expression, for decades the political parties were 'modern princes', today they are no longer up to the task, at least in their recognised form. In the age of neoliberal biopolitics, the modern princes are our hearts and bodies. And, through its ends and its practices, neo-liberal romanticism shows itself to be one of the most sophisticated instruments of hegemony that have ever been invented.

In this respect, we see an increasing need for a cultur-ally elevated discussion not only on the political use of passions, but also on their effectiveness and on the active means of governing passions that could again open up the spaces of political imagination. This means focusing on passions not so much (or no longer) as an object of politics, but rather as a dimension decisive to rethinking a new political subjectivity. In this context, writing an 'alphabet of passions' is an ever more necessary task. Obviously, we do not think that this alone is sufficient. But it is clear that, in the face of the abuse of passions, a capacity to understand the world is insufficient if it repudiates the force of passion or views passions with haughty disdain. The only thing that can reactivate our understanding is an embrace of feelings, which should allow us to develop a political form able to dispute today's dominant commonplaces. Ultimately, this is simply a wager that politics is not doomed to being a mere experience of frustration; a wager that politics can return to the utopian kernel that accompanied its modern genesis; a wager that politics can be a place in which human beings feel that their power to transform their lives is not some blessing or miracle. Rather, it is a common passion that constantly reinvents what we call democracy.

Notes

Notes to Introduction

1 See A. Tarpino, *Geografie della memoria: Case, rovine, oggetti quotidiani*, Einaudi, Turin 2008.

2 N. Ginzburg, 'Prefazione', in G. Falaschi (ed.), *La letteratura partigiana in Italia, 1943–1945*, Editori Uniti, Rome 1984, p. 8.

3 For a masterly introduction to the world of contemporary politics, see J. Dunn, *The Cunning of Unreason: Making Sense of Politics*, HarperCollins, London 2000.

4 'Anything that we can call morality today merges into the question of the organization of the world ... we might even say that the quest for the good life is the quest for the right form of politics, if indeed such a right form of politics lay within the realm of what can be achieved today.' Quoted in Judith Butler, 'Can one lead a good life in a bad life?', *Radical Philosophy* 176 (2012), p. 10.

Notes to Chapter 1

1 Hoggett and Thompson, who have recently edited a volume that reviews the effects of the affective turn on political theory, call for a distinction between *emotions*, feelings that are more conscious 'insofar as they are anchored in language and meaning', and *affects*, 'the more embodied, unformed and less conscious dimension of human feeling'. This is an unusual ascription of roles, for in general it is the emotions, not the affects, that are identified with the passions and their less conscious and controllable dimension. This is just one example of the myriad of often contradictory definitions that have been proposed. See P. Hoggett and S. Thompson (eds), *Politics and the Emotions: The Affective Turn in Contemporary Political Studies*, Bloomsbury Academic, London 2012, pp. 2–3. See also N. Demertzis (ed.), *Emotions in Politics: The Affect Dimension in Political Tension*, Palgrave Macmillan, Basingstoke 2013.

2 S. James, *Passion and Action: The Emotions in Seventeenth-Century Philosophy*, Oxford University Press, Oxford 2000, p. 52. Here as elsewhere we are greatly indebted to her work.

3 N. Ginzburg, *Prefazione*, in G. Falaschi (ed.), *La letteratura partigiana in Italia, 1943–1945*, Editori Uniti, Rome 1984, pp. 8–9.

4 Seneca, *De ira* 1.5, in Aubrey Stewart's stranslation. On the political function of anger in the contemporary age, see P. Sloterdijk, *Rage and Time*, Columbia University Press, New York 2010.

5 See F. Cerrato's fine book *Un secolo di passioni e politica: Hobbes, Descartes e Spinoza*, DeriveApprodi, Rome 2012.

6 'This decaying sense, when wee would express the thing it self, (I mean fancy it selfe,) wee call Imagination, as I said before: But when we would express the decay, and signifie that the Sense is fading, old, and past, it is called Memory' (T. Hobbes, *Leviathan*, Barnes & Noble, New York 2004, p. 5).

7 Ibid., p. 91.

8 'This personal gratification, which Descartes defines as the affect of Generosity (*Générosité*), is reached when there matures an adequate understanding of the possible relationship between subjective desires and their real chances of realisation. This emotional condition becomes a premise on the basis of which we can elaborate an idea of society, in which we can reduce the rate of potential conflict and the risk of war to a minimum' (Cerrato, *Un secolo di passioni*, p. 70). In a still unsurpassed book on this theme, Remo Bodei suggests that we abandon the image of the Stoic Descartes, dedicated to a severe form of self-control, and privilege instead the relationship between the rational control of passions and a life dedicated to joy: 'it is symptomatic that the series of six fundamental passions (wonder, love, hatred, desire, sadness and joy) begin with wonder and do not include fear' (R. Bodei, *Geometria delle passioni: Paura, speranza, felicità: Filosofia e uso politico*, Feltrinelli, Milan 1991, p. 266).

9 But how is this possible? Deleuze explains this well in one of the finest (and most renowned) passages dedicated to Spinoza in recent times: 'Spinoza sets out one of the most fundamental questions in his whole philosophy ... by saying that the only ques-

tion is that we don't even know what a body is capable of, we prattle on about the soul and the mind and we don't know what a body can do. But a body must be defined by the ensemble of relations which compose it, or, what amounts to exactly the same thing, by its power of being affected. As long as you don't know what power a body has to be affected, as long as you learn like that, in chance encounters, you will not have the wise life, you will not have wisdom' (G. Deleuze, *On Spinoza*: text available at https://bit.ly/2EtGXq6).

10 'If two men make an agreement with one another and join forces, they can do more together, and hence, together have more right over nature, than either does alone. The more connections they've formed in this way, the more right they'll all have together' (B. Spinoza, 'Political Treatise', in *Collected Works*, vol. 2.2, Princeton University Press, Princeton 2016, p. 513).

11 On the former, see Karl Friedrich Schinkel's paintings *Gotischer Dom am Wasser* (1813) and *Gotische Kirche auf einem Felsen am Meer* (1815). On the latter, see M. Hollein, C. Béret, R. Koolhaas et al., *Shopping: A Century of Art and Consumer Culture*, Hatje Cantz, Ostfildern-Ruit 2002.

12 C. Pateman, *The Sexual Contract*, Stanford University Press, Stanford, CA 1988.

13 C. Pateman and E. Grosz (eds), *Feminist Challenges: Social and Political Theory*, Routledge, New York 2013, p. 4.

14 S. Ahmed, *The Cultural Politics of Emotion*, Edinburgh University Press, Edinburgh 2004, p. 3. See also J. B. Elshtain, *Public Man, Private Woman:*

Women in Social and Political Thought, Princeton University Press, Princeton 1981.

15 E. Pulcini, *La cura del mondo: Paura e responsabilità nell'età globale*, Bollati Boringhieri, Turin 2009, p. 65. The author rightly emphasises that this distinction between public passions and private sentiment has its origin in Rousseau.

16 'No doubt, wherever public life and its law of equality are completely victorious, wherever a civilization succeeds in eliminating or reducing to a minimum the dark background of difference, it will end in complete petrifaction' (H. Arendt, *The Origins of Totalitarianism*, Meridian, New York 1958, p. 302).

17 W. Shakespeare, *Hamlet*, Act 3, scene 2, lines 177–9.

18 On this, see U. Frevert, *Emotions in History: Lost and Found*, Central European University Press, Budapest 2011.

19 Thomas Aquinas, *Summa theologiae* 2.1, Question 17, Article 7.

20 N. Bobbio, *In Praise of Meekness: Essays on Ethics and Politics*, Polity, Cambridge 2000.

21 Ibid., p. 26 (translation altered).

22 Ibid., p. 24.

Notes to Chapter 2

1 C. Schmitt, *Political Romanticism*, MIT Press, Cambridge, MA 1986.

2 Ibid., p. 20.

3 A. A. Schmidt, *Byron and the Rhetoric of Italian Nationalism*, Palgrave Macmillan, New York 2010, p. 39.

4 Naturally, 'sympathy' is not a concept of romantic *invention.* In his 1759 *Theory of Moral Sentiments,* Adam Smith had contended that sympathy, defined as the capacity to immerse oneself in other people's realities and feelings, is the mechanism that regulates the ethical relations between individuals.

5 Cited in F.C. Beiser, *Enlightenment, Revolution and Romanticism,* Harvard University Press, Cambridge, MA 1992, p. 235.

6 W. Wordsworth, 'The world is too much with us', 1–4, in idem, *Lyrical Ballads and Other Poems,* Wordsworth Editions, Ware 2003, p. 184.

7 Episode cited in G. Hauch, 'Women's spaces in the men's revolution of 1848', in D. Dowe et al. (eds), *Europe in 1848: Revolution and Reform,* Berghahn, Oxford 2001, p. 645.

8 For sharp reflections on the limiting character of republican virtue (i.e. limiting at women's expense) in the tradition running from Rousseau to Mazzini, see A. Banti, *L'onore della Nazione,* Einaudi, Turin 2005 pp. 58 ff.

9 See N.L. Rosenblum, *Another Liberalism: Romanticism and the Reconstruction of Liberal Thought,* Harvard University Press, Cambridge, MA 1987, pp. 22 ff.

10 G. Leopardi, 'Memorie del primo amore', in idem, *Opere,* edited by S. Solmi. Ricciardi, Milan 1956, pp. 855 ff.

11 I. Berlin, *Roots of Romanticism* (2nd edn), Princeton University Press, Princeton 2013, p. 151.

12 See M. Walzer, *Politics and Passion: Toward a More Egalitarian Liberalism,* Yale University Press, New Haven, CT 2006.

13 M. Nussbaum, *Political Emotions: Why Love Matters for Justice*, Harvard University Press, Cambridge, MA 2013, pp. 1–24. By 'history of liberalism' Nussbaum means the history of political liberalism or of liberal democracies.

14 'Great democratic leaders, in many times and places, have understood the importance of cultivating appropriate emotions (and discouraging those that obstruct society's progress toward its goals). Liberal political philosophy, however, has, on the whole, said little about the topic' (ibid., pp. 3–4).

15 E. Enriquez, *Dall'orda allo stato: Alle origini del legame sociale*, Il Mulino, Bologna 1986; S. Freud, *Mass Psychology*, Penguin, London 2004, p. 90.

16 A. Ehrenberg, *La société du malaise*, Odile Jacob, Paris 2010; C. Türke, *Erregte Gesellschaft: Philosophie der Sensation*, C. H. Beck, Munich 2002; H. Rosa, *High-Speed Society: Social Acceleration, Power, and Modernity*, Pen State University Press, University Park 2010; Byung-Chul Han, *The Burnout Society*, Stanford University Press, Stanford 2015.

17 For a complete analysis of the full array of alternative economic proposals, see R. Mancini, *Trasformare l'economia: Fonti culturali, modelli alternativi, prospettive politiche*, Franco Angeli, Milan 2014.

18 C. Campbell, *The Romantic Ethic and the Spirit of Modern Consumerism*, Alcuin Academics, London 2005, p. 4.

19 For Foucault, neoliberalism's *strength* in relation to socialism lies precisely in the fact that it possesses a 'governmental reason': M. Foucault, *The Birth of Biopolitics*, Palgrave Macmillan, London 2008, pp. 11–2.

20 M. Foucault, 'About the beginning of the hermeneutics of the self: Two lectures at Dartmouth', *Political Theory* 21.2 (1993): 198–227, here p. 203.

21 The political narrative seems to be concerned only with these first two techniques. An excess of attention to the first – the analysis of techniques that produce objects – is one of the reasons why there is today no political expertise outside political economy and why the economists are the only experts called on to answer political questions. An excess of attention to the second – the analysis of techniques that allow us to use systems of signs – is apparent in the emphasis with which we define the quality of a politician almost exclusively in terms of communication. The exemplary model of the good politician would be an individual who can communicate well and is able to reduce the complexity of questions to the uniformity of classic political economy. Could we not say that the impotence of politics is linked to the historical obsolescence of such a model?

22 Foucault, *Birth of Biopolitics*, pp. 68–9.

23 The intersection, in the neoliberal age, between politics, economics and the passions has been the subject of a constant flow of critical studies. Just by way of example, we can cite C. Marazzi, *Il posto dei calzini: La svolta linguistica dell'economia e i suoi effetti sulla politica*, Bollati Boringhieri, Turin 1999; F. Lordon, *La société des affects: Pour un structuralisme des passions*, Seuil, Paris 2013.

24 In this sense, any attempt to 'domesticate' the passions within modern normativity seems pointless. These attempts – first among which is obviously that of Nussbaum – seem not to have taken note of the

structural transformations of democracies and of the ideological use that they now make of passions. Thus the discourse on how to insert the positive passions within the ideal of a liberal democracy seems to be ideological, itself, that is, it sounds like a justification for democratic regimes whose only use of passions is functional to the expansion of inequalities and the oligarchical restriction of the spaces of politics. Domesticated passions seem to serve to drill us in a democracy without conflict. S.R. Krause does not seem immune to this tendency either, in her *Civil Passion: Moral Sentiment and Democratic Deliberation*, Princeton University Press, Princeton 2010 pp. 48–77.

25 Foucault, *Birth of Biopolitics*, p. 147.
26 A. Smith, *Theory of Moral Sentiments*, I, I, 1 (text available at https://bit.ly/1kuRPay).
27 M. Aime and A. Cossetta, *Il dono al tempo di Internet*, Einaudi, Turin 2010.
28 T. Streeter, '"That deep romantic chasm": Libertarianism, neoliberalism and the computer culture', in A. Calabrese and J. C. Burgelman (eds), *Communication, Citizenship, and Social Policy: Re-Thinking the Limits of the Welfare State*, Rowman & Littlefield, New York 1999, pp. 49–64 (the image of the 'deep romantic chasm' is taken from Whitman).
29 Pamuk's reference to Aristotle's theory of time appears in his *Museum of Innocence*, Alfred A. Knopf, New York 2009, p. 287.
30 W. Wordsworth, *The Two-Part Prelude* (1798–9), Part 1, in idem, *Selected Poetry*, edited by N. Roe. Penguin, Harmondsworth 1992, p. 106, ll. 288–9.

See also Lord Byron, *The Island, or Christian and his Comrades*, canto III, section iv: 'scarce five minutes pass'd before the eyes; | But yet *what* minutes! Moments like to these; | Rend men's lives into immortalities' (p. 52 in the 1839 edn, John Hunt, London).

31 Gérard de Nerval, cited in M. Löwy and R. Sayre, *Révolte et mélancolie: Le romantisme à contrecourant de la modernité*, Payot & Rivages, Paris 1992, p. 30.

32 H. Rosa, *Accelerazione e alienazione: Per una teoria critica del tempo nella tarda modernità*, Einaudi, Turin 2015, p. 15.

33 On this, see A. Penzin, *Rex exsomnis: Sleep and Subjectivity in Capitalist Modernity*, Documenta, Kassel 2012; J. Crary, *24/7: Late Capitalism and the End of Sleep*, Verso, London 2014.

34 Foucault, *The Birth of Biopolitics*, p. 133.

Notes to Chapter 3

1 M. Banerjee, 'Sacred elections', in *Economic and Political Weekly* 42.17 (2007), p. 1561.

2 For an impassioned reflection on the 'dysfunctions' of democracy, see J. Dunn, *Breaking Democracy's Spell*, Yale University Press, New Haven, CT 2014.

3 'What we are confronted with is the prospect of a society of laborers without labor, that is, *without the only activity left to them. Surely, nothing could be worse*' (H. Arendt, *The Human Condition*, University of Chicago Press, Chicago, IL 1958, p. 5).

4 We might note Hofstadter's famous recognition that '[t]he application of depth psychology to politics, chancy though it is, has at least made us acutely

aware that politics can be a projective arena for feelings and impulses that are only marginally related to the manifest issues' (R. J. Hofstadter, *The Paranoid Style in American Politics*, Vintage Books, New York 2008, p. xxxiii).

5 T. Pievani, *Evoluti e abbandonati*, Einaudi, Turin 2014, pp. 3–6.

6 In fact there is nothing scandalous or intrinsically new in the insistence to portray the politician's affective life as the triumph of some passions over others. If we study the geneaology of political parties as well as the well-known tendency towards oligarchy suggested by Michels, we also find the less renowned but equally indicative 'origins' hypothesis advanced by Clastres: that is, the idea that the caste of politicians emerged as an institutionalisation of the warrior caste, in its attempt to save itself from the death to which it would otherwise be destined. It would, then, seem almost inevitable for political relations to be regulated like small wars. See R. Lourau, 'Lo stato incosciente', in E. Colombo (ed.), *L'immaginario capovolto*, Elèuthera, Milan 1987, pp. 121–2. On this overall question, see especially M. Revelli, *Finale di partito*, Einaudi, Turin 2013.

7 'Power is war, the continuation of war by other means' (M. Foucault, *Society Must Be Defended*, Picador, New York 2003, p. 15).

8 Pievani, *Evoluti e abbandonati*, p. 4.

9 Niccolò Machiavelli, *The Prince*, chapter 15, in William K. Marriott's translation.

10 For a compelling reconstruction of the distinction between Machiavelli and Machiavellianism,

see M. Senellart, *Machiavellismo e ragion di stato*, Ombre corte, Verona 2014.

11 *Enciclopedia o dizionario ragionato delle scienze, delle arti e dei mestieri ordinato da Diderot e da d'Alembert*, edited by P. Casini, Laterza, Rome-Bari 2003 p. 521 (the piece is attributed to Diderot). French language version at https://bit.ly/2Hhz89U.

12 J. S. Mill, *Conditions on Representative Government*, text available at https://bit.ly/2HiHDBB.

13 M. Weber, 'Politics as a Vocation', in idem, *From Max Weber: Essays in Sociology*, Routledge, London 2001, p. 123.

14 Ibid., p. 114.

15 For this widely discussed theme, we simply refer the reader to A. Honneth, 'Recognition as Ideology', in B. Van den Brink and D. Owen (eds), *Recognition and Power: Axel Honneth and the Tradition of Critical Social Theory*, Cambridge University Press, Cambridge 2007; and to E. Pulcini, 'Patologie del Riconoscimento: Riconoscere che cosa?', in *Quaderni di teoria sociale* 8 (2008): 135–55.

16 '[T]he experience of being loved constitutes a necessary precondition for participation in the public life of a community. This thesis becomes plausible when it is understood as a claim about the emotional conditions for successful ego-development: only the feeling of having the particular nature of one's urges fundamentally recognized and affirmed can allow one to develop the degree of basic selfconfidence that renders one capable of participating, with equal rights, in political will-formation' (A. Honneth, *The Struggle for Recognition*, Polity, Cambridge 1995, p. 38).

17 Weber, 'Politics as a Vocation', p. 115.

18 This is one of the main aspects of the 'disarming of critique' (L. Boltanski and E. Chiapello, *The New Spirit of Capitalism*, Verso, London 2006, pp. 343 ff.).

19 Baruch Spinoza, *Ethics*, 3, 26.

20 See R. De Monticelli, *Al di qua del bene e del male*, Einaudi, Turin 2015.

21 The bureaucratisation of politics concerns not only the increasingly active role of bureaucracies. Voters also seem to have fallen into this 'passion for bureaucratisation', which identifies political discourse with the discourse coming from politicians. See M. Weber, *Economy and Society*, Bedminster, New York 1968, p. liii.

22 Weber, 'Politics as Vocation', p. 107.

23 P. Rosanvallon, *Counter-Democracy: Politics in an Age of Distrust*, Cambridge University Press, Cambridge 2008.

24 A. Hirschman, *Shifting involvements: Private interest and public action*, Princeton University Press, Princeton, NJ 1982.

25 G. Zagrebelsky, *Imparare democrazia*, Einaudi, Turin 2005.

26 Ibid., p. 39.

27 'The art of not being governed or better, the art of not being governed like that and at that cost. I would therefore propose, as a very first definition of critique, this general characterization: the art of not being governed quite so much' (M. Foucault, *The Politics of Truth*, Semiotext(e), Los Angeles, CA 2007, p. 45).

28 With these words we are invoking the ten com-

mandments of Franco Arminio's *Per una politica commossa* (http://comune-info.net/2016/01/polit ica-commossa).

29 D. F. Wallace, *Infinite Jest*, Abacus, London 1996.

Notes to Chapter 4

1 A. Gramsci, 'La famiglia', *Il grido del popolo*, 9 February 1918. On the family and the poltics of everyday life, see P. Ginsborg, *Il tempo di cambiare: Politica e potere della vita quotidiana*, Einaudi, Turin 2004, pp. 107-58.

2 See D. Ballas, D. Dorling and B. Hennig, *The Social Atlas of Europe*, Policy Press, Bristol 2014, passim; also O. Löfgren, 'The great Christmas quarrel and other Swedish traditions', in D. Miller (ed.), *Unwrapping Christmas*, Clarendon Press, Oxford 1995, pp. 217-34, on Christmas-time tensions in Swedish families.

3 A. Rosmini, 'Discorso in occasione del matrimonio del fratello Giuseppe', in idem, *Scritti sul matrimonio*, Forzani, Rome 1902, p. 329.

4 D. W. Winnicott, *The Child, the Family, and the Outside World*, Penguin, Harmondsworth 1971. See also the enlightening article by S. Alexander, 'Primary maternal preoccupation: D. W. Winnicott and social democracy in mid-twentieth-century Britain', in S. Alexander and B. Taylor (eds), *History and Psyche: Culture, Psychoanalysis and the Past*, Palgrave Macmillan, New York 2012, pp. 149-72.

5 On engagement and wedding songs, see C. D. Worobec, *Peasant Russia: Family and Community in the Post-Emancipation Period*, Princeton University Press, Princeton 1991, pp. 134-6 and 171.

6 D. Smith, *Dear Octopus*, Heinemann, London 1938, p. 120.

7 Plato, *Republic* 5, 464c–d, in Benjamin Jowett's translation.

8 See Martha Nussbaum's analysis in *Upheavals of Thought: The Intelligence of Emotions*, Cambridge University Press, Cambridge 2003, p. 359.

9 Aristotle, *Politics* 2, 1261ᵃ18–19, in Harris Rackham's translation.

10 Ibid., 1262ᵃ13–14.

11 Ibid., 7, 1330ᵃ3–6.

12 Ibid., 4, 1295ᵇ25.

13 Ibid., 8, 1337ᵃ21–31. While in the *Republic* Plato sought to abolish the family, in the *Laws* he retained it, albeit with notable restrictions. The domestic cult had to be limited and meals had to be consumed in common, not only by men and boys but also by women and girls. Little time was spent in the family apart from nighttime. Newman comments that in the *Laws* the family 'would seem to escape abolition only to be condemned to a somewhat shadowy existence' (W. A. Newman, *The Politics of Aristotle*, vol. 1, Oxford University Press, Oxford 1887, p. 180).

14 *Mencius*, Chinese University Press, Hong Kong 1979. See also Wei-Ming Tu, 'Probing the "three bonds" and "five relationships" in Confucian humanism', in W. Slote and G. De Vos (eds), *Confucianism and the Family*, SUNY, Albany, NY 1998, pp. 121–36; G. Therborn, *Between Sex and Power: Family in the World, 1900–2000*, Routledge, London 2004, p. 135.

15 *Mencius*, pp. 307, 309. Explanatory note in the original.

16 F. Fukuyama, *Trust: The Social Virtues and the Creation of Prosperity*, Hamish Hamilton, London 1985, p. 86.
17 O. Lang, *Chinese Family and Society*, Yale University Press, New Haven, CT 1946, especially pp. 54–6 and 181–92 (on nepotism).
18 Text from https://www.marxists.org/reference/archive/mao/selected-works/volume-1/mswv1_2.htm.
19 See K. A. Johnson, *Women, the Family and Peasant Revolution in China*, University of Chicago Press, Chicago, IL 1983, pp. 93 ff.
20 For an analysis of the various phases of birth control in China, see S. Greenhalgh and E. Winckler, *Governing China's Population: From Leninist to Neoliberal Biopolitics*, Stanford University Press, Stanford, CA 2005.
21 See R. A. Thaxton Jr, *Catastrophe and Contention in Rural China: Mao's Great Leap Forward, Famine and the Origins of Righteous Resistance in Da Fo Village*, Cambridge University Press, Cambridge 2008.
22 P. Nolan, *The Political Economy of Collective Farms: An Analysis of China's Post-Mao Rural Reforms*, Polity, Cambridge 1988, pp. 83 ff.
23 David Barboza's investigation of the Wen family's wealth (*New York Times*, 26 October 2012) won him the Pulitzer Prize.
24 'We fritter away our commitment, our energy and our courage for the benefit of the family, but for society and for *the state we have little left over*' (N. Bobbio, 'La fine della prima Repubblica', *L'Europeo*, 52, 28 December 1990, p. 107).

25 E. Banfield, *The Moral Basis of a Backward Society*, Free Press, Glencoe, IL 1958, p. 10.

26 A. Signorelli, 'L'incertezza del diritto: Clientelismo politico e innovazione nel Mezzogiorno degli anni '80', *Problemi del socialismo*, 2–3 (1988), p. 258.

27 L. Franchetti, *Condizioni politiche e amministrative della Sicilia*, Donzelli, Rome 1993 [1876], p. 40.

28 Plato, *Protagoras* 325c–d, in W.R.M. Lamb's translation (see *Plato in Twelve Volumes*, vol. 3, Harvard University Press, Cambridge, MA 1967).

29 C. Salvagni, 'La scuola dei genitori', *La Repubblica*, 29 January 2016.

30 S. James, *Passion and Action: The Emotions in Seventeenth-Century Philosophy*, Oxford University Press, Oxford 2000, pp. 189–91.

31 R. Putnam, *Bowling Alone: The Collapse and Revival of American Community*, Simon & Schuster, New York 2000, pp. 21 ff.

32 Thatcher archive COI transcript: visit http://www.margaretthatcher.org/document/106689. The interviewer was Douglas Keay.

Notes to Postscript

1 Article from *Corriere della Sera*, 8 May 1974, reprinted in Primo Levi, *Opere*, vol. 1, Einaudi, Turin 1997, p. 1187. He continued, in this same article: 'one can reach such a condition in many ways, not necessarily by means of terror and police intimidation, but also by withholding or manipulating information, by polluting the judicial system and by paralysing the school system'.

2 See the long article on CasaPound by Tobias Jones in the *Guardian* of 22 February 2018.

Index

Index

Index

Index

Index

love 4, 9, 12–14, 23, 31–3,
      38, 115–16, 128
  collective 107
  familial 11, 95–109
  romantic 43
love of nature 41, 44
love stories 57
Löwy, M. 135n(31)

Machiavelli, Niccolò 71, 73,
      74, 136–7n(10)
  The Prince 37, 72–3,
      136n(9)
Machiavellianism 37,
      65–75, 76, 78, 109–10,
      136–7n(10)
mafias 110
mailing lists 58
Mancini, R. 132n(17)
Mao Zedong 104, 105
  see also Great Leap
      Forward
Marazzi, C. 133n(23)
Mauriac, FranAois 97
Mazzini, G. 131n(8)
Mencius 101–2,
      140n(14–15)
methodological decentring
      84
Michels, R. 136n(6)
middle ages 13, 31
Mill, John Stuart 39, 42,
      75–6, 137n(12)
Miller, D. 139n(2)

Napoleon Bonaparte 42
nationalism 40, 81
  fanatical 42

Nazism 37–9, 121–2
  SS death squads 1
  see also neo-Nazis
neo-fascists 122
neoliberal passions 79, 92,
      124
  contest between education
      in inclusive passions and
      93
  seductive power of 4–11
  undiscussed, unanimous
      acceptance of 28
neoliberal romanticism 9,
      26, 32, 53, 55, 124
  consumer capitalism and
      44–52
  ends and practices of 125
  impotence of realism in
      the face of 60
  oriented towards seducing
      and distracting families
      115
neo-Nazis 122
Nerval, Gérard de 135n(31)
Newman, W. A. 140n(13)
Nolan, P. 141n(22)
Novalis (G. von Hardenberg)
      41
Nussbaum, Martha 44–5,
      132n(13), 133–4n(24),
      140n(8)

oligarchies 54, 64, 91,
      134n(24)
  political 66
  well-known tendency
      towards 136n(6)
  worn-out 68

Index

opposites 30, 31, 50
fundamental series of 13
Owen, D. 137n(15)

Pamuk, Orhan 57, 134n(29)
parliaments 42, 122
vulnerability to pressure
from lobbying 75
participation 55, 56, 77, 86
active 63
containers for attracting
68
dutiful 62
impassioned 61
limitation of the power of
66
mass 61
necessary precondition for
137n(16)
opportunity for
abundance of 59
political oligarchies
instrumentalise 66
representation and 87, 88,
91
rituals of 66
usable space of 64
widened 87
see also political
participation
participatory democracy 74
myth of 86
passions
absolutisation of 33, 35
active function of 26–31
alphabet of 119
alternative 3–4
ancestral 122

ancient history of 12–15
anti-political 89
attention as passion for
one's own 84
base 4
brief and intense moments
of 42
capacity to regulate 21
civic 38
combination of states of
mind and 121
common 24, 81, 114;
specific 82
conformism of 93
constant articulation of 34
consumerist 3
contamination of 87
control over 7, 118;
rational 128n(8)
countervailing 112
crisis of 63
dangerous influence/
supremacy of 19, 39
debate on 12–38, 113, 121
democratic 82
depoliticised 53
discipline and 44
domesticating 55,
133–4nn(24)
double crisis of 82–91
driving 122
elementary materialism of
16
eliminating the
naturalisation of 28
emotions and 19, 127n(1)
evaluation within specific
contexts 35

Index

Index

Index

Index

Index